SING FOR FREEDOM

The Story of the Civil Rights Movement Through Its Songs

Compiled and Edited by
Guy and Candie Carawan

A SING OUT PUBLICATION
Bethlehem, Pennsylvania

Music Editor: **Ethel Raim**
Editorial Assistance (We Shall Overcome): **Julius Lester**
Book Design (Freedom Is a Constant Struggle): **Ken Thompson & Jean Hammons**
Publication Director (new edition): **Peter Blood-Patterson**
Cover Photo: **Ken Thompson**

A major portion of the author's royalties for this book are being donated to the We Shall Overcome Fund to support cultural work in the South in the spirit of the freedom movement.

ISBN: 0-86571-180-1 (paperback)
ISBN: 0-86571-179-8 (hardbound)

Orders and inquiries should be directed to the publisher, **Sing Out Corporation**, at **P.O. Box 5253, Bethlehem, PA 18015-5253; (215) 865-5366**. Book trade orders and inquiries may be directed to New Society Publishers at 4527 Springfield Avenue, Philadelphia, PA 19143; (215) 382-6543.

INTRODUCTION TO THE NEW EDITION

In the spring of 1989, Appalachian miners striking the Pittston Coal Company were singing "We Shall Overcome." In China, where a massive campaign for democracy by students and workers has just been put down, students were photographed with "We Shall Overcome" on their headbands and T-shirts. Bishop Desmond Tutu has used the song as he tries to help people in the United States envision what his country is going through in its painful struggle toward equality and justice. This powerful song, which came originally out of the black church in the southern United States, was adapted and used in the labor movement, and rose to international prominence as the theme song of the civil rights movement. It lives today. It is but the best known of more than eighty songs which were developed and spread in the South and around this country between 1960 and 1965.

The civil rights movement has been described by some as the greatest singing movement this country has experienced. The freedom songs came out of the historical experience and the creativity of southern black communities. There are many kinds and ranges of moods. Two especially important ones are the old, slow-paced spirituals and hymns that sing of hope and determination, and rhythmic jubilee spirituals and bright gospel songs that protest boldly and celebrate victory. Many of these songs have new or revised words to old tunes.

Having witnessed the civil rights era, most of us take for granted the notion of adapting well-known songs to situations of the present. It wasn't always so. Bernice Reagon has pinpointed the moment in 1962, at a mass meeting in Albany, Georgia, when she understood:

Charlie Jones looked at me and said, "Bernice, sing a song." And I started "Over My Head I See Trouble in the Air." By the time it got to where "trouble" was supposed to be, I didn't see any trouble, so I put "freedom" in there. That was the first time I had the awareness that these songs were mine and I could use them for what I needed. (from Eyes on the Prize, *the companion volume for the PBS television series on the civil rights movement)*

We offer you here a collection of freedom songs. These songs emerged out of the campaigns against racism and injustice in the early 1960s and were originally published in two volumes by Oak Publications, We Shall Overcome (1963) and Freedom Is A Constant Struggle (1968). There is every reason to publish them again now. They are still useful songs (they are easily adapted to new situations) and they embellish the history of the U.S. civil rights movement in a concise and poetic manner. We want to explain a little about how they grew, how they spread, and how they are still around to be used in struggles throughout the world in the late 1980s.

The civil rights movement was the result of more than a century of suffering, and decades of careful and often dangerous work to address that suffering, in black communities in the South. The black church was the heart of these communities – a source of spiritual and physical sustenance – and singing was central to the worship experience. The original songs spoke mainly of personal salvation, and surviving the trials and tribulations of a harsh life on earth. Movement songs did not just automatically appear as people began to organize, march, and call attention to discrimination. Rev. C.T. Vivian explains:

At the beginning of the movement, we really didn't have any music that we could call "movement music." We had church music, but remember that it was largely a young movement; it was a movement of change. It needed something to fit it. We also didn't realize how important a dynamic music would be to a movement. That was the beginning of a movement and we didn't know what was necessary and what wasn't. We weren't thinking about it in terms of "what is going to inspire us?"

When we did start seeking songs to use at mass meetings, the only thing we had among us that had any sense of life to it was church music. And some of the church music didn't fit at all. For instance, I was giving a movement speech once, and the choir followed with "I'll Fly Away." Now that didn't fit at all. In fact it was a direct contradiction to what I was saying. How much different it could have been if they had followed with a movement song that was also religious.

I don't think we had ever thought of spirituals as movement material. When the movement came up, we couldn't apply them. The concept has to be there. It wasn't just to have the music, but to take the music out of our past and apply it to the new situation, to change it so it really fit. (All quotes from C.T. Vivian are from a 1983 interview with the editors.)

So how did this begin to happen? One place it happened was at the Highlander Folk School in Monteagle, Tennessee. Highlander was one of the gathering places during the early days of the movement. Weekend after weekend in the early 1960s, community leaders and activists from across the South came to share information, to strategize and to plan, to bolster each others' spirits as they returned home to confront segregation.

We were based at Highlander for those years and could build on what had been learned there during the Labor Movement – that singing could be a strong unifying force in struggle, and that commonly known songs, particularly southern gospel and religious songs with repetitive stanzas adapted to the situation, were most effective. For many years Zilphia Horton had worked with grassroots community people coming to Highlander. She drew from them their favorite songs and helped them change a word or two or shape them slightly differently to fit the situation in their home community (often a union campaign). She also taught songs that she knew from different parts of the South, from around the country and from abroad. In the 1940s and '50s she carried songs from Highlander out to picket lines across the South and brought songs back from various union struggles.

Others helped with this process. Zilphia, her husband Myles, and Lee Hayes (who spent a period of time working with her) knew, for example, John Handcox in the Southern Tenant Farmers Union – who contributed effective union songs based on familiar melodies. His "Roll the Union On," "There's Mean Things Happening in This Land" and "Raggedy, Raggedy Are We" all became widely known in the South and are still sung today. Pete Seeger had been in contact with Zilphia and with Highlander. His repertoire, as he sang with progressive movements in the North, included many songs from the South. He came to Highlander to share his music, and in 1945 carried away from the school a labor version of "We Shall Overcome" which had been used by striking Food and Tobacco Union workers in Charleston, S.C.

Guy had been greatly influenced by Pete, struck by his exciting way of playing the banjo and his collection of songs from grassroots Americans. In 1959, on Pete's suggestion, he came to work at Highlander and tried to carry on Zilphia's way of working with people. He met with groups gathered there and learned their songs, helping to adapt them to the movement activity in their communities. He also began to travel out to visit the people he had met and found himself leading singing in mass meetings and at civil rights conferences. It did not take long for the notion of adapting songs to catch on and to hit its stride. C.T. Vivian again:

The first time I remember any change in our songs was when Guy came down from Highlander. Here he was with this guitar and that tall frame, leaning forward and patting that foot. I remember James Bevel and I looked across at each other and smiled. Guy had taken this song, "Follow the Drinking Gourd;" and I didn't know the song, but he gave some background on it and boom, that began to make sense. And little by little, spiritual after spiritual after spiritual began to appear with new words and changes – "Keep Your Eyes on the Prize, Hold On" or "I'm Gonna Sit at the Welcome Table." Once we had seen it done, we could begin to do it.

As the movement spread, the songs began to spread. Nashville had one of the first citywide campaigns against segregation, and songs emerged there to suit the sit-ins. There was a talented quartet of ministerial students at American Baptist Theological Seminary who introduced humorous and satirical rhythm and blues and rock and roll songs to the growing repertoire of spirituals and gospel songs suitable to the movement. Bernard Lafayette and James Bevel in particular would carry the Nashville songs on to many new situations in the coming years. Candie was an exchange student at Fisk University in the spring of 1960 and learned firsthand about the power of singing in tough situations, including jail cells. Our courtship took place in these heady times.

During that same spring at a conference in Raleigh, NC, students from across the South met and organized the Student Nonviolent Coordinating Committee (SNCC). It was a chance for students from dozens of southern cities to compare experiences, plan a coordinated campaign for the coming months and, in the midst of discussing and strategizing, to sing together. When they went home, they took with them many newly adapted freedom songs. At the same time, the older adult organization, Southern Christian Leadership Conference (SCLC), was pulling its membership together at South-wide conferences. Many movement preachers could claim songleading as one of their skills. The notion of adapting songs was making its way into their churches, particularly at mass meetings, which were now a regular part of community life.

In 1961, the freedom rides swept through the South. When more than 350 freedom riders from many parts of the nation decided to stay in jail in Mississippi for the summer, the freedom song repertoire got a big boost. This was probably one of the most important periods for the development of movement singing. Most of the freedom riders spent 40 days in jail and had lots of time to learn and sing together all the best songs that had come from many areas. All the Nashville songs were taken over and the repertoire enriched by songs that people from CORE contributed. CORE, the Congress on Racial Equality, had started the freedom rides and had been joined by riders from other organizations when they were violently attacked and the rides were in danger of being canceled.

A lot of songs were made up or adapted in jail and the freedom riders carried them back to their home communities. We think of Cordell Reagon, for example, who began singing freedom songs as a teenager in Nashville during the sit-ins, came to Mississippi as a freedom rider, and then moved on to Albany, Georgia, where he taught songs and helped form the SNCC Freedom Singers.

Of course, jail time was spent in other ways too. There was plenty of time for strategizing and planning future campaigns. Parchman Penitentiary became a training ground for civil rights workers who would then go forward to new communities in southwest Georgia, in Mississippi, and in the black belt of Alabama.

As you read and sing through the collection of songs gathered in this book, you will trace the spread of the movement and you will notice how the songs evolved and grew to include the older traditional styles of deep South communities like Albany, Georgia, and the Mississippi delta; modern gospel compositions from Birmingham; songs written by individual songwriters like Matthew Jones or Len Chandler; and more angry songs as the movement made its way into northern inner cities. Bernice Reagon has been the preeminent historian of civil rights music. She reminds us again of the link between the Afro-American church in southern communities and the evolution of freedom songs:

Most of the singing of the civil rights movement was congregational; it was sung unrehearsed in the tradition of the Afro-American folk church...The core song repertoire was formed from the reservoir of Afro-American traditional song performed in the older style of singing. This music base was expanded to include most of the popular Afro-American music forms and singing techniques of the period. From this reservoir, activist songleaders made a new music for a changed time. Lyrics were transformed, traditional melodies were adapted and procedures associated with old forms were blended with new forms to create freedom songs capable of expressing the force and intent of the movement.

Again and again, it was to the church that the movement activists came for physical protection and spiritual nurturing – the very structure developed by the Afro-American community for the survival of its people. The church provided the structure and guidance for calling the community together; it trained the singers to sing the old songs and gave them permission to create new ones. (from Black Music Research Journal, vol. 7, 1987.)

As the movement with its music spread throughout the South, it also came north and made an impact on the country as a whole. The SNCC Freedom Singers began to travel outside the South, raising money and telling about the movement. Pete and Toshi Seeger set up programs for them at college campuses across the country. Pete had been south several times, learning firsthand what was taking place and spreading the news in his own concerts throughout the world. He had brought Bob Dylan to Mississippi; Joan Baez came to the South too, and sang for integrated audiences. The Newport Folk Festival, which drew crowds of 60,000 people in 1964 and 1965, included groups of freedom singers from Albany, Selma, and Birmingham on the program. Ralph Rinzler, Alan Lomax, and Theodore Bikel all came south to meet the movement activist/songleaders and to find ways for them to share their experiences with a wider public.

There were a series of music workshops, planned and organized in the South, which also fed into this cross-fertilization. The first had been at Highlander in the summer of 1960 and brought together songleaders from some of the very early civil rights campaigns (including Montgomery and Nashville) with northern protest singers and songwriters.

In 1964 there was a much richer exchange which took place in Atlanta. Called a "Sing for Freedom," it was jointly sponsored by Highlander, SCLC and SNCC and organized by Bernice and Cordell Reagon, Dorothy Cotton, Andrew Young, and Guy. By this time there were powerful singing movements in Albany, Selma, Birmingham, several parts of Mississippi, and many smaller communities. Each movement was invited to send songleaders to teach and learn freedom songs. A small group of northern singer/songwriters were invited and those who came included Tom Paxton, Len Chandler, and Phil Ochs. Also invited to share experiences and songs were some older traditional southern artists – Bessie Jones and the Georgia Sea Island Singers, and Doc Reese, a Texas minister who had served time in the Texas prison system and who was a masterful singer of prison work songs.

Two more workshops in 1965 would follow this first Sing for Freedom – one in Edwards, Mississippi and one at Highlander. These gatherings, in addition to focusing on the current freedom culture also encouraged the reclaiming of a rich Afro-American past. Folklorists – Alan Lomax and Willis James, in particular – met freedom fighters at these conferences and intense discussions took place about the value of older cultural traditions to contemporary struggles. Several southern communities caught up in the freedom movement (in the Sea Islands, Mississippi, and Louisiana) began to sponsor local folk festivals. Bernice Reagon wrote to us recently that being with Bessie Jones, the Sea Island Singers, and Doc Reese in those early gatherings changed her life. Indeed she and others from the movement (we think of Worth Long, Julius Lester, Jerome Smith) have gone deeper and deeper into Afro-American culture since those days and have shared what they have learned with the country through albums, publications, and in Bernice's case, conferences and workshops at the Smithsonian Institution.

These days there is renewed interest in the civil rights movement and in the powerful singing that became such an integral part of the struggle. As we honor that history and try to build on it in our continuing quest for justice and equality in this country, it is worthwhile to remember that neither the movement nor its music arrived full-blown in the South. Each evolved step by step, creatively, as ordinary people in grassroots communities recognized problems and came together to confront them. Some institutions and many community leaders found ways to nurture the process, bringing people together to learn from one another, to pass along what they had learned until finally it moved a nation.

These songs should not be lost. Many were brought along into other movements which followed the civil rights movement. There's still plenty of work to be done and hopefully it will be accompanied by powerful singing.

I don't see anyone having struggle separate from music. I would think that a movement without music would crumble. Music picks up people's spirits. Anytime you can get something that lifts your spirits and also speaks to the reality of your life, even the reality of oppression, and at the same time is talking about how you can really overcome: that's terribly important stuff. —Rev. C.T. Vivian

Sing on. Sing for Freedom!

Guy & Candie Carawan
Highlander Center, New Market, Tennessee
June 1989

6

We recommend the following additional resources:

BIBLIOGRAPHY

Bernice Johnson Reagon, Voices of the Civil Rights Movement: Black American Freedom Songs, 1955-65. Includes 3-volume record set and extensive accompanying booklet, which represents a definitive history of this music.

Reagon, Songs of the Civil Rights Movement 1955-64: A Study in Culture History. PhD dissertation, Howard University, 1975.

Reagon, "Let the Church Sing Freedom," in Black Music Research Journal, vol. 7, 1987. Center for Black Music Research, Columbia College, Chicago IL.

Reagon, Contemporary Black American Congregational Song and Worship Traditions. Booklet from a conference at Smithsonian Institution, February 1989.

Reagon, "Songs That Moved the Movement," in Perspectives, Civil Rights Quarterly, Summer 1983.

Pete Seeger and Robert Reiser, Everybody Says Freedom, W.W. Norton, NY, NY, 1990.

DISCOGRAPHY: Documentary Collections by Guy and Candie Carawan

The Nashville Sit-in Story, Folkways FH 5590.

We Shall Overcome: Songs of the Freedom Riders & the Sit-ins. Folkways FH 5591.

Freedom in the Air. SNCC Records.

Birmingham, Alabama, 1963. Folkways FD 5487.

The Story of Greenwood, Mississippi, 1965. Folkways FD 5593.

Sing for Freedom, 1990. A new 70-minute compilation of songs from the above recordings available as Folkways SF 40032. May be ordered as CD or cassette from Roundup Records, P.O. Box 154, N. Cambridge, MA 02140 (phone 800-443-4727) or directly from Sing Out (see inside back cover).

OTHER DISCOGRAPHY

Jimmy Collier and Rev. Frederick Douglas Kirkpatrick, Everybody's Got a Right to Live, Broadside BR 308.

Matt Jones, Then and Now. Relevant Records.

Moses Moon, Movement Soul: Sounds of the Freedom Movement in the South, 1963-4. Folkways FD 5486.

Bernice Johnson Reagon, Voices of the Civil Rights Movement: Black American Freedom Songs, 1955-65. 3-volume record set (see above under bibliography.)

Pete Seeger, We Shall Overcome (Carnegie Hall Concert, June 1963), Columbia Records.

Freedom Songs: Selma, Alabama. Folkways FH 5594.

The Sit-In Story: The Story of the Lunchroom Sit-in. Folkways FH 5502.

We Shall Overcome: Documentary of the March on Washington. Folkways FH 5592.

Sit-in Songs: Songs of the Freedom Riders, CORE. Dauntless Records, DM 4301.

FILMS AND VIDEO

We Shall Overcome. Public Broadcasting System special on the history of the song, by Jim Brown, 1988.

Eyes on the Prize. Six-part PBS series on the history of the Civil Rights Movement, Blackside Productions, 1986.

Songs of the Southern Freedom Movement

WE SHALL OVERCOME!

Compiled by Guy and Candie Carawan for
The Student Non-Violent Coordinating Committee

TABLE OF CONTENTS
We Shall Overcome

SIT-INS (1960) 13

We Shall Overcome 15
We Are Soldiers 16
I'm Gonna Sit at the Welcome Table 18
They Go Wild Over Me 20
How Did You Feel? 22
Everybody Sing Freedom 24
We Shall Not Be Moved 25
This Little Light of Mine 27
You'd Better Leave Segregation Alone 30
Dog, Dog 32
I Know (We'll Meet Again) 37
Ballad of the Student Sit-ins 40
Moving On 42

FREEDOM RIDES (1961) 43

Which Side Are You On? *(James Farmer)* 45
Freedom's Comin' and It Won't Be Long 46
Get Your Rights, Jack 48
Hallelujah, I'm A-Travelin' 50
If You Miss Me from the Back of the Bus 52
Hully Gully 53
Buses Are A-Comin', Oh Yes 54
Parchman Parodies *(new words to 14 songs)* 55

ALBANY, GEORGIA (1961-62) 59

Ain't Gonna Let Nobody Turn Me Round 62
Oh Pritchett, Oh Kelly 64
Sing Till the Power of the Lord Comes
    Down 66

Come and Go with Me to That Land 68
Certainly, Lord 69
I'm On My Way to the Freedom Land 70
I'm So Glad 73
Oh Freedom 74
Over My Head *(Bernice Johnson Reagon)* 77
Walkin' for Freedom Just Like John 78

VOTER REGISTRATION (1962-63)
Fayette Co. TN, sw GA, Miss. Delta, & AL 79

One Man's Hands 81
Woke Up This Morning with My Mind on
    Freedom 83
Get On Board, Little Children 86
Come By Here 87
Fighting For My Rights 88
Been Down Into the South 90
We'll Never Turn Back 93
Ballad of Herbert Lee 96
The Hammer Song 98

GREENWOOD, BIRMINGHAM
Through the march on Washington, 8/63 99

Guide My Feet While I Run This Race 102
Bull Connor's Jail 103
Ballad for Bill Moore 104
Hard Travelin' 106
Ninety-Nine and a Half Won't Do 107
Keep Your Eyes on the Prize 111

INTRODUCTION (From the 1963 edition)

On February 1, 1960, four Negro college students sat at a lunch counter in Greensboro, North Carolina, and asked for service. Their single act has grown into a great historic movement that has stirred the conscience of the South and of the nation. This collection of songs is meant to help document that growth and give support to the testimony of those who have seen the movement in action – that it has developed a singing spirit that moves the hearts of all who hear. But to really convey this takes more than the printed page. It must be experienced. It will help, then, when going through this book, to at least try to imagine what is at stake for some of the singers and what some of the situations are in which the songs are sung. It is hoped that the supplementary notes and photographs will help.

Freedom songs today are sung in many kinds of situations: at mass meetings, prayer vigils, demonstrations, before freedom rides and sit-ins, in paddy wagons and jails, at conferences, workshops and informal gatherings. They are sung to bolster spirits, to gain new courage and to increase the sense of unity. The singing sometimes disarms jail guards, policemen, bystanders and mobs of their hostilities.

These songs tell a special kind of short history of many major developments and events of the nonviolent movement in the South. First begun as a protest against segregated lunch counters, the movement has gone on to include restaurants, libraries, museums, art galleries, churches, courtrooms, parks, beaches, swimming pools, laundromats, employment, transportation and voter registration. As each of these new areas has come under attack, new ways of dramatizing the issues to the public have been needed. The Negro students have played the major role in initiating these new forms of demonstrations. The same is true of the new singing spirit and repertoire of freedom songs. The students have been responsible for making up most of the new lyrics and singing new life into the old songs. Just as Negro adult communities have rallied in support of the student demonstrations, so have they been influenced by their songs and sung them at mass meetings, demonstrations, and other gatherings.

Today student workers, many of them veterans of successful integration campaigns in other areas of the South, are attempting to carry their knowledge and experience to some of the places in the deep South that need help. With them goes their singing spirit, and it is proving to be a great asset in their work. They continue to make up new songs about their experiences, and the body of freedom songs keeps growing.

New songs about events in Albany and some of the surrounding counties in southwest Georgia, about the voter registration work going on in many small towns in the Mississippi delta, about new student demonstrations in places like Talladega and Gadsden, Alabama, keep appearing regularly. This book represents just the beginning of the story. There will be many more songs and chapters to be written in this struggle for human dignity.

NOTES ON THE SONGS

The song versions given in this book should not be taken as absolutely definitive. It should be realized that these words and tunes are sung with some variation from area to area and person to person. Words are often adapted to new situations and new verses ad-libbed on the spot. Also, the improvisational style in which they are sung cannot be completely captured by orthodox musical notation. Anyone familiar with the musical characteristics of Negro folk style in spiritual and gospel singing, in blues and rock 'n' roll, will know that these transcriptions represent only a bare skeleton of what is actually being sung. Good singers will subtly vary the tune – bending notes, delaying or anticipating the beat, and adding their own vocal decorations. Singers are continually improvising new harmony parts. Some very imaginative bass parts have evolved. The Freedom Singers from Albany, GA, exemplify this improvisational style – combining the best of the old-time religious singing style with modern gospel and rock 'n' roll music.

Pete Seeger has said: "One woman on the Selma march saw me trying to notate a melody, and said with a smile, 'Don't you know you can't write down freedom songs?' – which has been said by everyone who ever tried to capture Negro folk music with European music notation. All I can do is repeat what my father once told me: 'A folksong in a book is like a photograph of a bird in flight.'" We hope that you will also freely adapt and improvise on these songs.

— **Guy and Candie Carawan**

SIT-INS

Stand—Ins

Wade—Ins

Kneel—Ins

Etc.

It was a chilly February first in 1960 when a handful of Negro students staged a sit-in at the Woolworth lunch counter in Greensboro, N.C. Within a week the sit-ins had spontaneously spread to Durham, Winston-Salem and Fayetteville and then swept into Charlotte, High Point and three other North Carolina cities. On the 11th the sit-ins erupted in Hampton, Virginia and on the 28th, 80 students were arrested during the first sit-ins in Nashville, Tennessee. On that same day, white and Negro students in New York City began massive picketing of the Woolworth stores. By the end of this first month, students in Los Angeles and Philadelphia started their picket lines as did Detroit students on March 5. On March 13, 2,000 students met at Yale to map support for the sit-ins and Woolworth stores were being picketed in most major cities of the nation.

In the South, hundreds of students had been arrested in less than a month. Tear gas had been used against 1,000 students peacefully marching in Tallahassee. Students had been herded at gun point into hastily built stockades in Orangeburg.

Since the first sit-in, thousands of students have been arrested and jailed. Many still in high school have faced tear gas, guns, brutal beatings, extended prison terms and expulsions from school. But the peaceful revolution could not be stopped.

excerpt from the 1963 War
Resisters League Calendar

VERSE

My moth-er ____ was a sol-dier, she had her hand on the gos - pel plow, ____ but one day she got old, ____ could-n't fight ____ an-y more, but she stood there and fought on an- y - how, Oh, Oh, ____ D.C.

Chorus:
We are soldiers in the army
We've got to fight although we have to cry
We've got to hold up the freedom banner
We've got to hold it up until we die.

I'm glad I am a soldier, I've got my hand on the gospel plow
But one day I'll get old, I can't fight anymore
I'll just stand here and fight on anyhow.

My mother was a soldier, she had her hand on the gospel plow
One day she got old, couldn't fight anymore
But she stood there and fought on anyhow.

I know I've been converted, and of this I am not ashamed
I was standing right there at the station
When the holy ghost signed my name.

I'm Gonna Sit at the Welcome Table

Adaptation of traditional song by members of SNCC

"When I first came to Nashville, I learned that there was only one movie theatre in that city, the capital of Tennessee, to which Negroes could go without having to enter through a back door or an alley entrance and climbing up to the ceiling or the balcony. I noticed that the lives of the Negro students in Nashville were, for the most part, spent on campus ... simply be- cause there was no place to go. They didn't have the right to sit at a lunch counter or do anything else any other citizen of Nashville could do. I couldn't believe that the children of my class- mates would have to be born into a society where they had to believe that they were inferior."

— Diane Nash

I'm gonna walk the streets of glory,
I'm gonna walk the streets of glory
  one of these days, hallelujah,
I'm gonna walk the streets of glory,
I'm gonna walk the streets of glory
  one of these days.

I'm gonna tell God how you treat me...

I'm gonna get my civil rights ...

I'm gonna sit at Woolworth's lunch
  counter ...

They Go Wild Over Me

Tune: "Popular Wobbly"
Words: Candie Anderson

"My stomach always hurt a little on the way to a sit-in. I guess it's the unexpected. There was so much we didn't know early in February, 1960, when the sit-ins first started in Nashville. Will the sit-ins accomplish anything? Will non-violence work? What happens when demonstrators are put in jail?

I was an exchange student at Fisk, living in the dorms and attending classes with Negro students. The biggest question for me was the rather lonely one of what can a white student do? What would my presence at the lunch-counter mean? Would I alienate and enrage the community to a greater extent than the Negro students? Or would it show that this is more than a Negro problem? I didn't know . . .

During the demonstrations I found myself and the other few white students singled out by the crowds, called different names and eventually even segregated in the Nashville City Jail. Eighty of us were arrested the first time. It was one of the first instances where large numbers of students went behind bars, and we found that singing was truly good for the spirit. For two white girls, alone in a cell and only in sound's reach of the other students, the music offered a bond of friendship and support." — Candie Anderson

This parody is an adaption of the old parody, The Popular Wobbly, from the days of the I.W.W. It originally was a popular tune entitled They Go Wild Over Me.

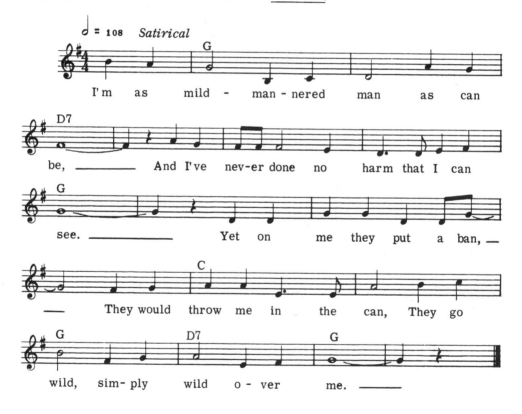

♩ = 108 *Satirical*

I'm as mild - man - nered man as can be, _____ And I've nev-er done no harm that I can see. _____ Yet on me they put a ban, ____ ___ They would throw me in the can, They go wild, sim- ply wild o - ver me. _____

I'm as mild mannered man as can be
And I've never done no harm that I
    could see
Yet on me they put a ban
They would throw me in the can
They go wild, simply wild over me.

Oh the manager he went wild over me
When I went one afternoon and sat for
    tea
He was breathin' mighty hard
When his pleas I'd disregard
He went wild, simply wild, over me.

Then the judge he went wild over me
And I plainly saw we never could
    agree
So I let his nibs obey
What his conscience had to say
He went wild, simply wild, over me.

Then the jailer he went wild over me
Well he locked me up and threw away
    the key
In a segregated cage
I'd be kept, it was the rage
He went wild, simply wild, over me.

They go wild, simply wild, over me
I'm referring to the bedbug & the flea
They disturb my slumber deep
They would rob me of my sleep
They go wild, simply wild, over me.

Will the roses grow wild over me
When I've gone into that land that is
    to be
When my soul and body part
In the stillness of my heart
Will the roses grow wild over me?

Will my children go wild or go free
When it's time for them to go to town
    for tea
Will those bedsheet wearin' whites
Still yell "Down with Civil Rights"
Or will justice have come to
    Tennessee?

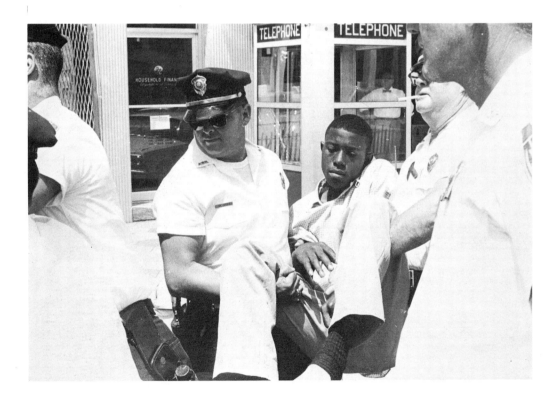

How Did You Feel?

Adaptation of traditional song by members of CORE

"We were crammed into a narrow hallway to await booking and I studied the faces around me. Many were calm and serious, some were relaxed, smiling, several were openly belligerent and a few were really frightened. But there was a unity -- a closeness beyond proximity.

"It was a shock then to be suddenly removed from this large coherent group and thrust into a lonely cell with only one other girl, the only other white female. We protested and inquired why we could not join the large group of Negro girls across the hall. The entire jail was segregated. Through our own small diamond-paned window we could see the corresponding window in the fellows' cell. There were nearly 60 boys crowded in there -- a cell the same size as ours which held two. When a face would smilingly press up against that window, we had our only visual contact with the group which had been so close that afternoon, and the previous Saturday afternoons when there had been sit-ins.

"The contact which became more real then was vocal. Never had I heard such singing. Spirituals, pop tunes, hymns, and even slurpy old love songs all became so powerful. The men sang to the women and the girls down the hall answered them. They shouted over to us to make sure we were joining in. Some songs that the kids had written or revised came out -- notably some rock-and-roll protests composed by four young Baptist preachers. Calypso songs and Ray Charles numbers made us dance in our roomy quarters and then all of us were singing spirituals -- 'Amen - Freedom.'

"We sang a good part of our 8 hour confinement that first time. The city policemen seemed to enjoy the singing. They even came up with a few requests. Our wardens actually welcomed us back when we returned to jail in a few days, going off our bond. We were a change from the Saturday night drunk who rarely sang."

— Candie Anderson

♩ = 66 *Rocking*

C

Oh tell me, how did you feel ___ when you

come out the wild-er-ness,   G7   come out the wild- er- ness,

C
come out the wild-er-ness,   how did you feel ___ when you
(Oh tell me,)

G7   C
come out the wild- er- ness,   Oh, praise ___ the Lord. ___

Oh tell me how did you feel when you
    come out the wilderness
    come out the wilderness
    come out the wilderness
Oh tell me how did you feel when you
    come out the wilderness
Oh praise the Lord.

Oh did you feel like fighting...etc.

Oh will you fight for freedom...

Oh will you walk the line...

Oh will you carry a sign...

Oh will you go to jail...

Oh will you join the CORE...

Everybody Sing Freedom

Adaptation of traditional song by members of SNCC

One of the first freedom songs to be sung in the Nashville jails during the Sit-ins was this adaptation of the spiritual, "Amen."

"The day of the first trials in Nashville a crowd of 2500 people gathered around city court house. Mostly they were Negroes who simply wanted to state by their presence there that they were behind the students and that they wanted justice. As we waited to go inside we sang:

"Amen, amen, amen, amen...
Freedom, freedom...
Justice...
Civil Rights..." etc.

I looked out at the curb where the police were patrolling, and caught one burley cop leaning back against his car, singing away -- "Civil Rights"... He saw me watching him, stopped abruptly, turned, and walked to the other side of the car." — Candie Anderson

Leader:

Everybody sing...

Fight for freedom...

Gain the Victory...

In the jail house...

In the cotton field...

In Mississippi...

All across the South...

We Shall Not Be Moved

Adaptation of traditional song

Talladega, Alabama: Bob Zellner describes a mass march on the mayor's office of about 200 Talladega College students protesting police brutality and collusion with the mob which beat demonstrators:

"The march was stopped about a block and a half from the campus by 40 city, county, and state policemen with tear gas grenades, billy sticks and a fire truck. When ordered to return to the campus or be beaten back, the students, confronted individually by the police, chose not to move and quietly began singing 'We Shall Not Be Moved.'"

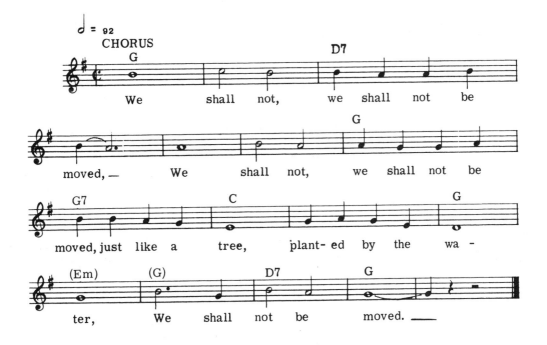

We shall not, we shall not be moved, — We shall not, we shall not be moved, just like a tree, plant- ed by the wa - ter, We shall not be moved. ___

We are fighting for our freedom, we
    shall not be moved,
We are fighting for our freedom, we
    shall not be moved,
Just like a tree, planted by the water,
We shall not be moved.

We are black and white together, we
    shall not be moved...

We will stand and fight together, we
    shall not be moved...

Our parks are integrating, we shall
    not be moved...

We're sunning on the beaches, we
    shall not be moved...

This Little Light Of Mine

Traditional song

"A song is to be sung. If it remains on the page, it is the same as a new automobile that is bought, placed in the garage and kept there.

"A song is to be sung. One's musical abilities may be limited, but there are no limitations to one's spirit. A musical note is a guide, but it alone does not make a song.

"A song is to be sung. One's musical abilities may be good for citizenship schools, mass meetings, etc. Some of the songs are to be shouted. Others are to be sung quietly, lived with and allowed to grow within you and with you. A song is to be sung."
— Julius Lester Highlander song book

"I believe that throughout our southland, and in other sections of the nation, too, we have been singing a song."
— Septima Clark - Echo in My Soul

CHORUS (or VERSE)

♩ = 204 *Very jubilant*

This-a lit-tle light of mine, — I'm gon-na let it shine, — (oh) — This lit-tle light of mine, — I'm gon-na let it shine, — (oh) — This lit-tle light of mine, — I'm gon-na let it shine, — Let it shine, — let it shine, — let it shine.

BRIDGE

The light that shines is the light of love, lights the dark-ness
from a-bove, it shines on me and it shines on you, —
shows what the power of love can — do, I'm gon-na
shine my light — both far and near, — I'm gon-na
shine my light both bright and clear, Where there's a dark cor-ner
in this land, I'm gon-na let my lit-tle light shine.

Chorus:
This little light of mine, I'm gonna
    let it shine
This little light of mine, I'm gonna
    let it shine
This little light of mine, I'm gonna
    let it shine
Let it shine, let it shine, let it shine

Bridge
The light that shines is the light of
    love, lights the darkness from
    above
It shines on me and it shines on you,
    and shows what the power of love
    can do
I'm gonna shine my light both far and
    near, I'm gonna shine my light
    both bright and clear
Where there's a dark corner in this
    land, I'm gonna let my little light
    shine.

Verses:

We've got the light of freedom, we're
    gonna let it shine...

Deep down in the South, we're gonna
    let it shine...

Down in Birmingham (Mississippi,
    Alabama, etc.), we're gonna
    let it shine...

Everywhere I go, I'm gonna let it
    shine...

Tell Chief Pritchett,...

All in the jail house...

Bridge
On Monday he gave me the gift of love
Tuesday peace came from above
Wednesday he told me to have more
    faith
Thursday he gave me a little more
    grace
Friday he told me just to watch and
    pray
Saturday told me just what to say
Sunday he gave me the power divine -
To let my little light shine.

You'd Better Leave Segregation Alone

New words by James Bevel & Bernard LaFayette

This parody of the rock n' roll song You Better Leave My Little Kitten Alone (recorded by Little Willie John) was made up and popularized in Nashville in the earliest days of the sit-ins by four students from American Baptist Theological Seminary, James Bevel, Bernard Lafayette, Joseph Carter, and Samuel Collier. They were also responsible for the next three songs in this book, two of them originals (Dog, Dog and I Know) and another parody (Moving On, adapted from Ray Charles recording).

♩ = 156

Freely

You'd bet-ter leave ———— se- gre-ga-tion a-lone—

slow gliss) In Strict Time (Guitar tacet)

be- cause they love se- gre- ga- tion like a

hound dog— loves a bone, ———— a bone.

1. Well I went down to the dime store to get my-self some eats, they
2. Well I went down to the dime store to get myself a coke, the

a bone   a bone   a

put me in the jail when I sat at them folks seat you'd better
wait-ress looked at me and she thought it was a joke, you'd better

bone ———————— a bone ———— you'd better

leave ———— se- gre- ga- tion a - lone

(Guitar Tacet)   E7

be- cause they love se - gre - ga- tion like a

D7

hound dog— loves a bone, ——— a bone.

a bone, a bone, — a bone, —— a

D7   A

bone, —— a bone, — a bone— be- cause they

E7   D7   A

love se - gre - ga - tion like a hound dog loves a bone,_ a bone.._

Dog, Dog

Words & music by James Bevel & Bernard Lafayette
© 1963 by Stormking Music Inc. All Rights Reserved.
Used by Permission.

"You know I lived next door to a man and he had a lot of children, and so did my dad, but we weren't allowed to play together because they were white. But we had two dogs. He had a dog and we had a dog. And our dogs would always play together... So we wrote this song."
— James Bevel

(Repeat throughout Tenor Solo

LEAD
(Tenor Solo)

1. black dog — I'm talk- in' 'bout a all 'em dogs
2. white dog—
3. rab- bit dog—
4. coon dog—

all — em dogs   All 'em dogs, Lord, Lord, All 'em

(No change in Tempo)

dogs a love - a my   dog and then - a   why can't

dog a love -a my   dog and then - a   why can't

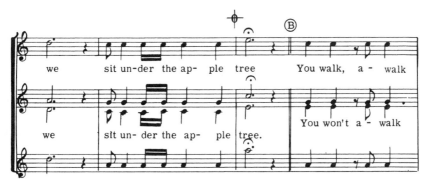

we   sit un-der the ap- ple tree   You walk, a - walk

we   sit un-der the ap- ple tree.   You won't a - walk

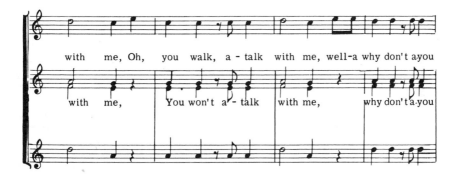

with me, Oh,   you walk, a - talk   with me, well-a why don't a you

with   me,   You won't a - talk   with me,   why don't a-you

33

hold my hand, — tell me a- you un-der-stand, now can't you

Div

hold my hand, tell me a- you un-der-stand, now can't you

see that you and me a-will- a be so a hap — py,

see that you and me a- will - a be so a-hap- py,

No Pause

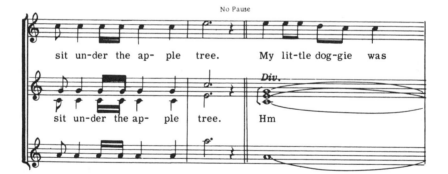

sit un-der the ap- ple tree. My lit-tle dog-gie was

Div.

sit un-der the ap- ple tree. Hm

play-in' one day Dog dog Dog dog an'

(whispered)

Dog dog (*ti — kaw — ka* | *ti ka*) Dog dog

down in the mea-dow by a bun-dle of hay   Dog dog

Dog dog *(ti-kaw - ka-*

Dog dog an- oth-er lit-tle dog- gie came a- long, _____

ti-ka)

Dog, dog   he said   let's get to-geth-er and a

(ti kaw-ka ti-ka) Dog dog

(half spoken)

eat this bone !   Dog dog   Dog dog well then - a

Dog dog *(ti kaw - ka ti ka)* Dog dog, well then a-

why can't we   sit un-der the ap-ple   tree.

Repeat B then A,
very fast: use the
following variation
for the solist.

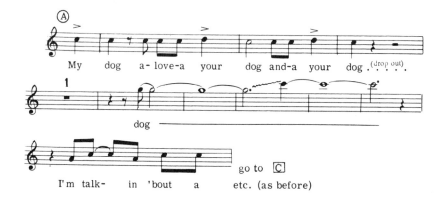

A

My   dog a-love-a   your   dog and-a   your   dog .(drop out).

1

dog

dog ⸺

I'm talk- in 'bout   a   go to C   etc. (as before)

CODA

tree. ⸺

tree ⸺

I Know

New words by James Bevel & Bernard LaFayette

This is one of the many freedom songs that Nashville students took to Jackson, Mississippi on the Freedom Rides. This song became one of the most popular. A couple of new verses were added and it became a favorite "goodbye" song.

* If there is only one soprano, disregard the lower part.)

Well when I left Missis-
sippi, oh, yes,
I travelled to Tennessee
There I worked with the
SNCC
Fighting for our dignity.

We've had fun in this
jail house, oh, yes,
And now we all must go
But we will be alone
after you've gone
My friend, I'm gonna
miss you so.

Ballad of the Student Sit-Ins

Words and music by Guy Carawan, Eve Merriam and
Norman Curtis

Since February 1, 1960, sit-in demonstrations have occurred in over three hundred cities in the USA. They have been mainly in the South and have involved Negro students accompanied by a small number of white sympathizers. Over 5,000 students have been to jail and many have suffered violence from hoodlums and police. Following the first sit-in in Greensboro, N.C., they spontaneously mushroomed all over the South where Negro student communities existed. After a year-and-a-half they had already brought about the desegregation of lunch counters in close to 150 Southern cities. In the North and in other parts of the country many people held demonstrations supporting the students in the South. In the last year-and-a-half, the emphasis has shifted to other forms of demonstrations such as Freedom Rides, the mass walks and praying at the City Hall in Albany, Georgia, voter registration work in deep South, Freedom Walks and mass demonstrations in Birmingham, Ala. At the same time, however, sit-ins have been popping up in new places, both North and South: Talladega, Huntsville, Gadsden, Ala.; Little Rock, Arkansas; Englewood, N.J.; Baltimore, or Route 40, etc...

The time was nine-teen six-ty, the place the U.S.A, that Feb-ru-a-ry first be-came a his-tory mak-ing day, from Greens-bo-ro a-cross the land the news spread far and wide that qui-et-ly and brave-ly youth took a gi-ant stride.

Chorus

Heed the call —— A-mer-i-cans — all, side by e-qual side, Bro-ther, —— sit in dig-ni-ty, — sis-ter sit in pride.

From Mobile, Alabama to Nashville,
  Tennessee
From Denver, Colorado to Washington
  D.C.
There rose a cry for freedom, for
  human liberty
Oh come along my brother and take a
  seat with me. (Cho.)

The time has come to prove our faith
  in all men's dignity
We serve the cause of justice, of all
  humanity
We're soldiers in the army with
  Martin Luther King
Peace and love our weapons, non-
  violence our creed. (Cho.)

This is a land we cherish, a land of
  liberty
How can Americans deny all men
  equality?
Our Constitution says we can't and
  Christians, you should know
Jesus died that morning so all mankind
  could know. (Cho.)

No mobs of violence and hate shall
  turn us from our goal
No Jim Crow laws nor police state
  shall stop my free bound soul
Three thousand students bound in jail
  still lift their heads and sing
We'll travel on to freedom like song
  birds on the wing. (Cho.)

Moving On

This freedom song is an adaptation by James Bevel and Bernard Lafayette of the original composition "Moving On" by Hank Snow, © 1950 (renewed) Unichappell Music Inc. All rights are reserved by the original publisher, Unichappell Music.

"I feel that each day in our classrooms we've been exposed to, we've talked about, learned about the democratic process and the ideas of democracy. But it makes me sick deep down inside to think that for over a hundred years the Negro has been abused, has suffered indignities bestowed upon him by the white man, has been told to go to the back, has been called inferior, and a second class citizen. I have found that I cannot continue to live with myself."

— Marion Barry

Se- gre- ga - tion's been here from time to time, ___ but we just ain't gon - na pay it no mind, — Well, it's mov- in' on, (keep mov-in' on) well, it's mov-in' on, (keep a' mov - in' on) Well, se - gre- ga - tion's been here, but now it's mov - in' on ___ (move on, move on, move on. . .)

Old Jim Crow's moving on down the
    track, he's got his bags and he
    won't be back
He's moving on... He's moving on...
Old Jim Crow's been here but now
    he's moving on.

Well I thought they was jiving about
    Jim Crow's gone
But I went down to his house and he
    sure wasn't home
He's moving on... He's moving on
Old Jim Crow's been here but now
    he's moving on.

42

FREEDOM RIDES

In mid-March 1961, the Congress of Racial Equality . . . announced that it would recruit a small, biracial group to ride Greyhound and Trailways buses from Washington, D.C. to New Orleans, La., with the purpose of challenging any segregation of interstate travellers encountered. On May 4, the Freedom Ride began, with 13 participants: six white, seven Negro, ranging in age from 18 to 61. The number fluctuated during the course of the Ride. Through Virginia, North and South Carolina, and Georgia there were few obstacles.

On May 14 came the events of Anniston and Birmingham. Mobs gathered, passengers were intimidated, a bus was burned and people were beaten while police were either inactive, not present, or strangely late in arrival . . . Many were hospitalized and the rest of the participants flew on to New Orleans and there disbanded.

But this was not to be the end . . . The Nashville Student Movement made the crucial decision to continue the rides in spite of the danger that awaited them. They took buses for Montgomery via Birmingham. They were jailed on arrival in the latter city. Released on May 19, they traveled on to Montgomery. That city received them with riots, which caused the intervention of federal marshals, and finally, a declaration by the Governor of martial law.

On May 24, the National Guardsmen of Alabama and the state police of Mississippi escorted them to Jackson, where they were arrested. In the next few months over 360 people, most college students, came to Jackson and spent time in prison to show their protest against segregated travel and their support of the Negro students already jailed there.

Their courage shamed political leaders into taking wavering steps toward securing equal justice before the law. On May 29, Attorney-General Kennedy requested the Interstate Commerce Commission to issue regulations at once requiring the full desegregation of buses and terminal facilities engaged in interstate travel. Finally on September 22 the I.C.C. issued such regulations with the directive that they must be posted aboard all buses and in all bus terminals by November 1.

–excerpted in part from the 1961 Southern Regional Council report on the Freedom Ride

Which Side Are You On?

Original verses by Florence Reese, new verses by James Farmer (CORE).

"I rewrote the old labor song by Florence Reece 'Which Side Are You On?' on the spur of the moment in the Hinds County Jail, after the Freedom Riders who were imprisoned there had been discussing and speculating about the attitude of local Negroes regarding the Freedom Rides. We had learned through trustees in the jail that most local Negroes were with us, but afraid to do anything because of fear of reprisals. They told us that, of course, there were a lot of Uncle Toms around and it was hard to tell who was and who was not."

— James Farmer

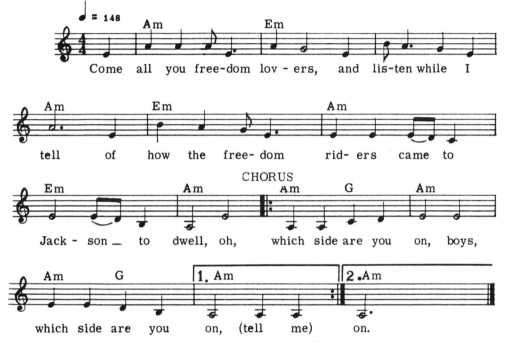

Come all you free-dom lov-ers, and lis-ten while I tell of how the free-dom rid-ers came to Jack-son _ to dwell, oh,

CHORUS

which side are you on, boys, which side are you on, (tell me) on.

My daddy was a freedom fighter and
   I'm a freedom son
I'll stick right with this struggle until
   the battle's won.

Don't 'tom for Uncle Charlie', don't
   listen to his lies
'Cause black folks haven't got a
   chance until they organize.

They say in Hinds County, no neutrals
   have they met
You're either for the Freedom Ride
   or you 'tom' for Ross Barnett.

Oh people can you stand it, tell me
   how you can
Will you be an Uncle Tom or will you
   be a man?

Captain Ray will holler 'move on', but
   the Freedom Riders won't budge
They'll stand there in the terminals
   and even before the judge.

Freedom's Comin' and It Won't Be Long

"The buses came into Anniston, Alabama on May 14, 1961.

The Greyhound bus station was closed, but a restless crowd of about 200 milled outside the depot. When the Greyhound carrying the "Freedom Riders" pulled in, the crowd turned into a mob. Rocks were hurled, windows smashed. When the bus managed to pull out, it was followed by a long line of automobiles. A slashed tire forced the bus to stop six miles outside of Anniston. The trailing convoy also stopped, and the mob grouped around the bus. More windows were broken, and a bomb was hurled through one of them. Smoke and flames forced the passengers to leave before the bus was destroyed by fire. Ten persons were taken to a hospital to be treated for smoke inhalation."

"In Birmingham, Alabama, another mob was waiting for the Trailways bus carrying the second group of 'Freedom Riders'. It was Mothers' Day; no police were on the scene. . . ."

— from a CORE report

46

Chorus: Freedom, Freedom, Freedom's comin' and it won't be long. (twice)

We took a trip down Alabama way,
    Freedom's comin' and it won't be
        long
We met much violence on Mothers'
        Day
    Freedom's comin' and it won't be
        long.

We took a trip on a Greyhound bus,
    ... etc.
To fight segregation, this we must
    ... etc.

Violence in 'bama didn't stop our
        cause ...
Federal marshals come enforce the
        laws ...

On to Mississippi with speed we go
        ...
Blue-shirted policemen meet us at the
        door ...

Judge say local custom shall prevail
    ...
We say 'no' and we land in jail ...

LAST VERSE

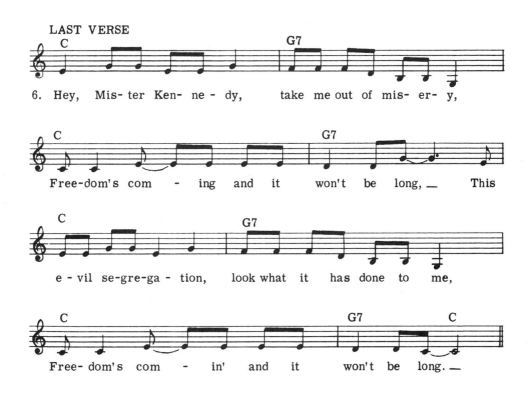

6. Hey, Mis-ter Ken-ne-dy, take me out of mis-er-y,

Free-dom's com - ing and it won't be long, — This

e - vil se-gre-ga - tion, look what it has done to me,

Free-dom's com - in' and it won't be long. —

Get Your Rights, Jack

New words by members of CORE. This freedom song is an adaptation of the original composition "Hit the Road, Jack" by Percy Mayfield, © 1961 (renewed) Tangerine Music (BMI). All rights are reserved by the original publisher, Tangerine Music.

"I remember one night at the jail, a voice called up from the cell block beneath us, where other Negro prisoners were housed. 'Upstairs!' the anonymous prisoner shouted. We replied, 'Downstairs!' 'Upstairs!' replied the voice, 'Sing your freedom song.' And the Freedom Riders sang. We sang old folk songs and gospel songs to which new words had been written, telling of the Freedom Ride and its purpose. Then the downstairs prisoners, whom the jailers had said were our enemies, sang for us. The girl Freedom Riders, in another wing of the jail, joined in the Freedom Ride songs."

— James Farmer

48

Chorus:
Get your rights, Jack, and don't be a
    'Tom' no more, no more, no
    more, no more
Get your rights, Jack, and don't be a
    'Tom' no more.

Oh CORE, oh CORE, don't you treat
    me this way
I'll take my freedom ride someday
Oh no you won't 'cause it's understood
You're an Uncle Tom and you're just
    no good.
Well I guess if you say so, I'll have to
    get my ticket and I'll go (That's right)

Oh Ross, oh Ross, don't you treat me
    this way
I'll get my civil rights someday
Oh no you won't 'cause it's understood
Your skin is black and you're just no
    good
Well I guess if you say so
I'll have to take it to the CORE.

Hallelujah I'm A-Travelin'

Tune: Harry McClintock ("Hallelujah I'm a Bum"), new words by Harry Raymond

Jackson, Mississippi — When the first 186 Freedom Riders returned en masse to be arraigned in court, a mass meeting was held the night before. Over 2500 Negroes came out in the rain to welcome them back and to show their support. When the Freedom Riders (over half of them white) walked into the crowded hall, the crowd stood and applauded. Never had Jackson Negroes seen such a mixed group nor such a state of comradeship between the races as existed between the young men and women who had ridden the buses, been arrested and experienced violence together.

The meeting of these Freedom Riders from all parts of the country was to be the beginning of a great spread of freedom song material. Housed together at Tougaloo College in Jackson, the Riders sang and shared their favorite songs and verses. From Jackson these songs went back to groups of people in every southern state, to churches and colleges in the north.

This song, "Hallelujah, I'm A' Travelin' " was picked up by a newspaper reporter in Columbia, Tennessee in 1946 at a trial following a riot. The reporter learned it from a Negro farmer who said, "Don't use my name."

Stand up and re-joice, a great day is here, We're rid-ing for free-dom and the vic-t'ry is near, Hal-le-lu-jah, I'm a-trav-el-in', Hal-le-lu-jah, ain't it fine, Hal-le-lu-jah, I'm a-trav-el-in' down free-dom's main-line.

Stand up and rejoice, a great day is
    here
We're riding for freedom and the
    victory is near.

Chorus:
Hallelujah I'm a travelin', hallelujah
    ain't it fine,
Hallelujah I'm a travelin' down free-
    dom's main line.

In 1954 our Supreme Court said, Look
    a here Mr. Jim Crow,
It's time you were dead.

I'm paying my fare on the Greyhound
    Bus line
I'm riding the front seat to
    Montgomery this time.

In Nashville, Tennessee I can order a
    coke
And the waitress at Woolworths knows
    it's no joke.

In old Fayette County, set off and
    remote
The polls are now open for Negroes to
    vote.

I walked in Montgomery, I sat in
    Tennessee
And now I'm riding for equality.

I'm travelin' to Mississippi on the
    Greyhound Bus line
Hallelujah I'm ridin' the front seat
    this time.

If You Miss Me From the Back of the Bus

Words: Carver Neblett Music: traditional

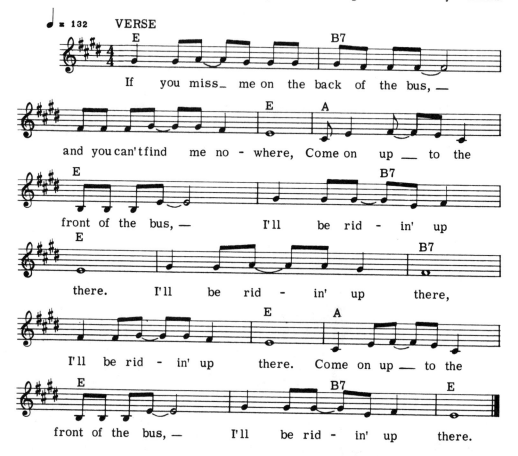

If you miss me from the front of the
   bus, and you can't find me nowhere,
Come on up to the driver's seat, I'll
   be drivin' up there.
I'll be drivin' up there, I'll be drivin'
   up there,
Come on up to the front of the bus,
   I'll be drivin' up there.

If you miss me from Jackson State,
   and you can't find me nowhere,
Come on over to Ole Miss, I'll be
   studyin' over there...etc.

If you miss me from knockin' on
   doors, and you can't find me nowhere,

Come on down to the registrar's room,
   I'll be the registrar there...etc.

If you miss me from the cotton field,
   and you can't find me nowhere,
Come on down to the court house,
   I'll be voting right there...etc.

If you miss me from the picket line,
   and you can't find me nowhere,
Come on down to the jail house, I'll be
   rooming down there...etc.

If you miss me from the Mississippi
   River, and you can't find me nowhere,
Come on down to the city pool, I'll be
   swimming in there...etc.

Hully Gully

New words by Marilyn Eisenberg

"On many evenings we sang rock 'n roll songs and danced the 'Twist', the 'Hully Gully' or the 'Watoosie' in our cells. I wrote this to the tune of one of the Hully Gully songs we were singing, and later we danced to it."
— Marilyn Eisenberg

♩ = 72

G

Well I went to Mis-si-sip-pi on the Grey-hound bus-line,

(Em) (G)

free-dom, free-dom ri-der, I went in-to the ter-min-al and

(Em) (G)

ev-ery-thing was fine, —— free-dom, —— free-dom ri-der,

D7 **C7**

sit-tin' in the wait-ing room, tryin' to get a tick-et,

G

may-be buy some cof-fee too. ____

The policeman said to me, Move out
    or move on.
      Freedom, Freedom Rider
I just kept a' sittin' there not doin'
    nothin' wrong,
      Freedom, Freedom Rider
I'm a Freedom Rider, she's a Free-
    dom Rider, you can be a Freedom
    Rider too.

They took me off to jail in a big black
    paddy wagon,
      Freedom, Freedom Rider
I sang all the way, my spirit wasn't
    draggin',
      Freedom, Freedom Rider
We Shall Overcome, and We Shall Not
    Be Moved, and Climbin' Jacob's
    Ladder too.

Well I went before the Judge and what
    did he say,
      Freedom, Freedom Rider
You have breached the peace now in
    jail you must stay,

      Freedom, Freedom Rider
Pay 200 dollars because you are so
    guilty, stay in jail for 4 months
    too.

I didn't pay my fine although I want to
    be free,
      Freedom, Freedom Rider
They carried me off to the
    penitentiary,
      Freedom, Freedom Rider
They put me in a cell and took away
    my mattress, Damn Yankee
    Agitator, you.

Now behind the bars I keep singin' this
    song,
      Freedom, Freedom Rider
Freedom's comin' and it won't be
    long,
      Freedom, Freedom Rider
I'm a Freedom Rider, he's a Freedom
    Rider, you can be a Freedom
    Rider too.

Buses Are A-Comin', Oh Yes

Adaptation of traditional song by members of SNCC

"I do not think that my participation in the Freedom Rides made an appreciable difference to the inevitably successful outcome of this struggle. Nor did I expect it to heal the wounds which the white majority has for decades inflicted on the Negro.

"I went to the South in inadequate obedience to the Biblical demand 'to do justly'. I went as a Jew who remembers the slavery of our forefathers in Egypt and who wants to obey the injunction to consider himself personally liberated from Egyptian slavery. I went as a Jew in response to the prophetic question 'Are ye not as the children of the Ethiopians to me, O children of Israel? saith the Lord.'

"My participation in the Freedom Rides was an act of faith in the validity of a moral act. I went because I needed to go."
— Henry Schwarzschild

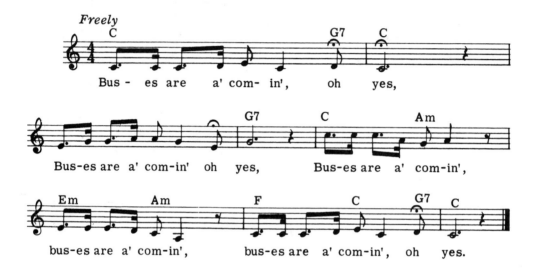

Bus - es are a' com- in', oh yes,

Bus-es are a' com-in' oh yes, Bus-es are a' com-in',

bus-es are a' com-in', bus-es are a' com-in', oh yes.

Buses are a comin', oh yes
Buses are a comin', oh yes
Buses are a comin', Buses are a
   comin',
Buses are a comin', oh yes.

Barnett, don't you hear them . . .

Freedom is a' comin' . . .

Comin' into Jackson . . .

Better get you ready . . .

Better get your ticket . . .

Ridin' in the front seat . . .

Rollin' across Dixie . . .

Parchman Parodies

"I like to think these songs had some small effect on others besides the Freedom Riders. Our matron, a formidable looking woman from Alabama, was at first very rough with the girls. She rarely spoke, and although we thought she was sympathetic to us as prisoners, we were sure she hated us as Freedom Riders. But some of the girls, in the true non-violent spirit, saw her as a human being and not as a symbol of authority and oppression. Little by little they began to speak to her. At first it was just "good morning" or "thank you", and then we began to joke with her and have longer and longer conversations. Before I left Parchman she was singing for us on our make-believe radio programs and was often heard humming our freedom songs."   — Marilyn Eisenberg

Several parodies to familiar tunes came out of the Freedom Rides. Those following were sent by Marilyn Eisenberg, a Freedom Rider from California:

Tune: Yankee Doodle

Freedom Riders came to town
Riding on the railway,
Mississippi locked them up
Said you can't even use Trailways.
  Mississippi, you are wrong,
  You've gone against the nation
  We'll keep coming big and strong
  And we'll end segregation.

Tune: On Top of Old Smokey

"Sometimes at night great big flying beetles and other bugs came in through the windows. We used our Bibles to swat them as there was nothing else available in the Parchman cells."

Way down in old Parchman
All covered with bugs
I lose all my sleep
'Cause the bugs are knee deep.

They come through the windows
They come from the john
They come in small armies
They keep marching on.

I stay up all night
With the book in my hand
And preach to the beetles
As I go slam, slam.

Two versions of The Battle Hymn of the Republic

1
Mine eyes have seen the coming of
  equality for all
And as the Freedom Riders we are
  answering the call
Even though we shall be placed behind
  old Parchman's prison wall
Segregation has to fall.
        Black and white shall ride
          together
        Black and white shall eat
          together
        Black and white shall live
          together
        Integration is for all.

        Black and white shall sit
          together
        Black and white shall learn
          together
        Black and white shall vote
          together
        Integration is for all.

2
Mine eyes have seen the disintegration
  of my underwear
Every time I put them on I seem to
  find another tear
Pretty soon I'll be walking round with
  my bottom bare
It's the Parchman fashion flair.
        Grab the sheets the men are
          coming
        Grab the sheets the men are
          coming
        Grab the sheets the men are
          coming
        It's the Parchman fashion
          flair.

Tune: Frere Jacques

"While in the Hinds County Jail we used to have shouted conversations with the male Freedom Riders imprisoned in a distant part of the jail. One day they didn't answer and we called out, 'Are you sleeping?' In a few minutes we were singing the following round which sprang up from that question."

Are you sleeping,
Are you sleeping,
Brother Bob?
Brother Bob?
    (... Atty. Gen. Robert Kennedy,
      of course)
Freedom Riders waiting,
Freedom Riders waiting,
Enforce the law,
Enforce the law.

Tune: Careless Love

"All was not high spirits and never-failing high morale. Some of us were pretty young and all of us had families and friends we missed very much. The humid heat, the bad food, and the lack of mail due to arbitrary censorship were bound to get us down sometimes. In a blue mood one day, I wrote this

song. MSU stands for Maximum Security Unit, and was the way we commonly referred to the area in which we were imprisoned."

I went to Jackson on a train
I went to Jackson on a train
I went to Jackson on a train
Lord, I won't do that again.

I had faith and love and pride
               (three times)
When I took that Jackson Freedom
    Ride.

They sent me to Parchman Farm
               (three times)
Where I could do no one no harm.

What they did they shouldn't do
               (three times)
They locked me up in MSU.

I miss my mama and my daddy too
               (three times)
I can't see them in MSU.

Cigarettes and candy too (three times)
When I get out of MSU.

Someday we shall overcome
               (three times)
But now I just want my sentence done.

Ralph Fertig — arrested on the Freedom Rides in Selma, Alabama wrote three of his own parodies:

Tune: <u>Streets of Laredo</u>

In a dirty and roach-ridden jail down
    in Parchman,
Packed into cells 'till they most
    overflow,
Are dozens of young folk of different
    races;
They're taking their places
To battle Jim Crow.

The Supreme Court decided that
    interstate travel,
Was free for all people in every state;
And they told Mississippi, "There's
    no segregating of folks who are
    waiting
To ride interstate."

But the laws of the nation have no
    application
To what transportation goes into that
    state;
As freedom is tested, young folks are
    arrested,
Arrested because
They would not segregate.

Now from Churches and classrooms
    all over the country,
With love in their hearts and resolve
    to be free,
More people on board,
Are riding straight toward
That jail where they put folks who
    seek dignity.

In a dirty and roach-ridden jail down
    in Parchman,
Packed into cells 'till they 'most
    overflow,
Are dozens of young folks of all
    diff'rent races;
They're taking their places
To battle Jim Crow.

Tune: <u>Dixie</u>

Oh, we're riding South and we're
    integrated,
New South' 'bout to be created;

Look ahead!
Look ahead!
Look Ahead Dixieland!
No more racist rule by Anglo-Saxon;
Black and White, we ride on Jackson;
Look Ahead!
Look Ahead!
Look Ahead, Dixieland!
We're riding forth through Dixie,
    today, hurray!
For liberty and dignity
We'll integrate all Dixie;
Hurray! Hurray!
We'll soon be free, in Dixie!

words by Ralph D. Fertig; 7/3/61

Tune: <u>Sweet Bye and Bye</u>

The elected officials all say,
"Things get better and better each
    day."
And when asked, "But how long will
    this take?"
They will answer with speeches so
    fake:

Chorus:
"You'll be free, Gradually,
Gotta' wait and cultivate for Liberty;
'Work and pray, and someday,
Folks will say, "You're O.K. to be
    free."

Mr. Lincoln in 1863
Told us then, we could start to be
    free;
But when we try to vote in our state,
They will tell us so sweetly to wait.

Chorus:

They will tell us to try and "be cool",
While our children are shut out from
    school;
And when we seek some freedom from
    fear,
All the "Moderates" sing loud and
    clear:

Chorus:

If you want to drive race hate away,
And you don't want to wait 'till you're
    grey,
You can stand up, or ride, or sit in
With your brothers of all tints of skin!

Then you'll see, You'll be free,
Take the course to be a force for
    liberty!
When you do what you pray
You'll find freedom and love right
    away!

words by Ralph D. Fertig 7/4/61

And other parodies:

Tune: Alloutte

All we ate here, think of all we ate
     here
All we ate here, think of all we ate
Think of all the peas we ate
Think of all the peas we ate
Peas we ate, peas we ate
Oh, all we ate here, think of all we
     ate here
All we ate here, think of all we ate.

Think of all the grits we ate . . . etc.
Think of all the pinto beans . . .
Think of all the turnip greens . . .
Think of all the corn meal mush . . .
Think of all the rice we ate . . .
Think of all the cabbage stewed . . .

and so on . . .

Tune: Down on the Freedom Line
        (Down by the Riverside)

Gonna take a long awaited ride
Down on the freedom line   (3 times)
Gonna take a long awaited ride
Down on the freedom line
I ain't gonna segregate no more.

Chorus:
I ain't gonna segregate no more . . .

Gonna ride in a first class way

Gonna take down those Jim Crow signs

Last Chorus:
I'm gonna integrate this time...

Tune: St. James Infirmary
        (words by William Bradford &
                 Weldon Rougeau —
                 both of CORE)

We went down to Mississippi on a
     Greyhound Senicruiser (ride)
A mob was there to greet us, they
     tried to make us the loser
        (God, it's a wonder that none of us
     died.)

We tried so hard to keep from crying,
     our hearts felt just like lead
But we'll keep on fighting until we're
     almost dead.

When we're gone and our children are
     all here, they'll be fighting for
     rights so dear
And someday the job will be done and
     our fight for freedom will be won.

Tune: Oh Mary Don't You Weep

Oh Riders don't you weep, don't you
     mourn (2)
Barnett's army got drownded, Oh
     Riders don't you weep.

Tune: The Midnight Special

If you ever go to Jackson, you'd better
     walk right
And you better not integrate and you
     better be white
Captain Ray will arrest you and he'll
     carry you down
Judge Spencer'll find you guilty then
     you're jail house bound.

(Captain Ray was the arresting officer
and Spencer the judge in Jackson.)

Tune: Jacob's Ladder

Do you, do you, want your freedom
                              (3 times)
Soldiers of the CORE (or brothers in
     this land)

Yes I, yes I, want my freedom . . .

Will you, will you, fight for freedom,
     etc.

Yes I'll, yes I'll, fight for freedom,
     etc.

Will you, will you, go to jail for
     freedom, etc.

ALBANY, GEORGIA

"Go down Kennedy
Way down in Albany
Tell old Pritchett
To let my people go."

In the city of Albany in the black belt of southwest Georgia, Negroes — young and old, working class and professional, college student and clergyman — are witnessing to the fact that they do not like segregation. Two weeks before Christmas, 1961, over 700 local Negro citizens were jailed as a result of the demonstrations at City Hall, protesting the jailing of Negro college students who used the bus and train stations on a non-segregated basis. Thousands of Albany Negroes participated in these peaceful demonstrations protesting the refusal of their city government and police force to comply with the new Interstate Commerce Commission's ruling stating that beginning November 1st, 1961, there could be no more discrimination in interstate transportation. On November 1st, and for the next six weeks, the Albany police continued to enforce segregation in the bus and train stations and arrested those students who used the white waiting rooms. The Federal Government took no apparent action to curb this violation. Then the mass demonstrations started.

Today in Albany the bus and train stations are desegregated; but this compliance with the I.C.C. ruling was not brought about by any action of the Federal Government but rather by the more than 700 Negroes who spent time in prison as a mass substitute for federal action.

Since the arrest of the original 736 in December, 1961, the number of those jailed has risen to over 1200. Reverend Martin Luther King, Jr. and Reverend Ralph Abernathy have been arrested on three different occasions and more recently 75 ministers of different faiths from New York City were arrested and jailed in Albany for praying at the court house. The original issue of whether or not the Albany City Government could prevent Negro citizens from exercising their federal rights in regard to inter-state travel has now changed to the even more basic issue of whether or not the Negro citizens of Albany (and the handful of white sympathizers) will continue to be denied their Constitutional right of peaceful protest under the first amendment by the Albany City Government. What originally started as a movement for a specific objective — that of unsegregated inter-state travel — has turned into a movement with larger objectives — those of full equality and human dignity. The demands of the Albany Movement today are an appointment to talk face-to-face with the City Commission about the eventual desegregation of all public facilities and the right of every eligible voter to register.

Albany is of special importance in the integration struggle. It is the first city in the deep South to have such wide support and participation in the Negro community across class and age lines demonstrating on a sustained basis for desegregation of all public facilities. Negroes all over southwest Georgia look to Albany as their hope. It is the major testing ground today for what might happen in many other areas of the deep South in the next few years.

Ain't Gonna Let Nobody
Turn Me Round

Adaptation of traditional song by members of the Albany Movement

This old spiritual was first introduced in Albany by Reverend Ralph Abernathy during the summer of 1962 when mass arrests and demonstrations errupted for the second time. He taught it one night to a mass meeting of the Negro community at Mount Zion Baptist Church. It immediately caught on and became widely used in the demonstrations. A nationally televised CBS documentary showed spirited students rhythmically clapping and singing "ain't gonna let Chief Pritchett turn me 'round" while the policemen picked them up, two to a student, and carried them into the paddy wagons.

". . . anybody who thinks this town is going to settle back and be the same as it was, has got to be deaf, blind, and dumb."

— A Negro woman in Albany, Ga.

Lead (tenor or alto)

Ain't gon-na let_ no-bod-y, Lord-y, turn me 'round,

turn me 'round, turn me 'round, Ain't gonna let no-bod-y, Lord-y,

turn me 'round, I'm gon-na keep on a-walk-in', Lord,

ye-ah,

keep on a-talk-in', Lord, march-ing up to free-dom land. —

Oh, ye-ah,

Ain't gonna let nobody turn me 'round,
    turn me 'round, turn me 'round,
Ain't gonna let nobody turn me 'round,
I'm gonna keep on a walkin', keep on a
    talkin'
Marching up to freedom land.

Ain't gonna let Nervous Nelly turn me   Ain't gonna let Z. T. . . .
    'round . . . (term applied to   (Z. T. Mathews, sheriff of Terrell
        typical segregationist)   County, Georgia)

Ain't gonna let Chief Pritchett . . .   Ain't gonna let no jail house . . .

Ain't gonna let Mayor Kelly . . .

                                               Ain't gonna let no injunction . . .
Ain't gonna let segregation . . .   (after a federal injunction pro-
                                                   hibiting further demonstrations)

Oh Pritchett, Oh Kelly

Music traditional, words by Bertha Gober & Janie Culbreath

In Albany the students were told when they were taken to some of the jails in the surrounding areas, "I don't want no damn singing and no damn praying." The authorities are beginning to realize the value of this singing in keeping the courage and morale of the students high. One student put it like this, "It helped to ease the knot in the pit of my stomach."

Janie Culbreth and Bertha Gober re-worked the spiritual "Oh Mary, Oh Martha" while in the Dougherty County Jail. They sing to Chief of Police Laurie Pritchett and Mayor Asa D. Kelly.

pray-in' in jail. 1. Bail's get-tin' high-er ———
2. Bond's get-tin' high-er ———

pray-in' in jail. ———

pray-in' in jail ———

bail's get-tin' higher, ———   Bail's get-tin' higher, ———
bond's get-tin' higher, ———   Bond's get-tin' higher, ———

pray-in' in jail ———

to [B]

bail's get-tin' higher ———   I
bond's get-tin' higher ———   I

pray-in' in jail ———   pray-in' in jail ——

Sing Till the Power of the Lord Comes Down

Adaptation of traditional song

SNCC field secretaries who helped start the demonstrations say that much of the success of the Albany Movement can be attributed to the role that singing played. They needed it to communicate with them. Through songs they expressed years of suppressed hope, suffering, even joy and love.

From the very beginning when SNCC organizers went into Albany and explained to dissatisfied local college students how they had worked for desegregation in other communities, they taught them the freedom songs. These students, raised in an area where old time singing is still prevalent in the churches, soon became the most exciting group of freedom singers in the South. After they were arrested for demonstrating at the bus and train stations, mass meetings were started. At first just a few people came, but as the arrests continued and news of these meetings with their exciting singing spread to the community, the meetings became packed and they had to use two churches to hold everyone. The young people taught their songs to the masses at every meeting and leaders of the newly formed Albany Movement talked and preached the ideas of non-violence and social action. In the old time singing and prayer sessions held at the start of each meeting the masses voiced their sentiments. Later on in the meeting they replied in confirmation to the words of the speakers and raised their voices again in song with the students in the new versions of their old songs.

Don't be a - fraid.   Sing till the

head   Now let us sing till the

pow - eer   of   the   Lord   comes   down.

pow - er   of   the   Lord   comes   down.

VERSE

This ___ world   is   one   great— bat - tle field   with

for - ces   all   ar - rayed, ___ But if   in   my   heart   I

do   not   yield,   Oh ___ I   will o - ver   come   some   day. ___

Come And Go With Me
To That Land

Adaptation of traditional song

"There has been more than one mass meeting in which the preacher has exhorted the soldiers of freedom, calling them to march for the cause of justice and truth, and they have answered, 'We are able.' Then in that very moment instead of a closing organ postlude and the polite shaking of hands, both preacher and a goodly part of the flock have taken up the marching song and streamed out of the church doors into the midst of the world, marching to jail singing."

— Vincent Harding & Slaughton Lynd — Crisis

Come and go — with me to that land, — come and go with me to that land. — Come and go — with me to that land — where I'm bound — (where I'm bound) — Come and go with me to that land, — come and go with me to that land, — Come and go with me to that land — where I'm bound. —

Come and go with me to that land,
　　come and go with me to that land,
Come and go with me to that land
　　where I'm bound;
Come and go with me to that land, oh
　　come and go with me to that land,
Come and go with me to that land
　　where I'm bound.

No Jim Crow in that land . . . etc.

No burning churches in that land . . .

There'll be singing in that land . . .   We'll all be free in that land . . .

There'll be freedom in that land . . .   All is well in that land . . .

No Chief Pritchett in that land . . .   There'll be peace in that land . . .

No more weeping, crying, bowing, etc.

Certainly, Lord

Adaptation of traditional song by members of CORE

♩ = 100 *Jubilant*

Well, have you been to the jail, ___ Cer-tain-ly, Lord,

Well, have you been to the jail, ___ Cer- tain- ly, Lord,

Well, have you been to the jail, ___ Cer- tain-ly, Lord, ___

Cer - tain - ly, cer - tain - ly, cer - tain- ly, Lord. ___

Well did they give you thirty days? . .

Well did you serve your time?

Well will you go back again?

Well will you fight for freedom?

Well will you tell it to the world?

Well will you tell it to the judge?

I'm On My Way
To The Freedom Land

Adaptation of traditional song

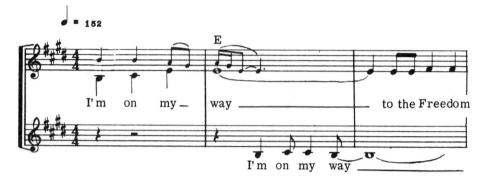

I'm on my way to the Freedom

I'm on my way

Land, I'm on my way

to the Freedom Land, I'm on my way

to Free-dom Land, I'm on my

to the Free-dom Land,

way to Free-dom Land,

I'm on my way to the Freedom Land,

                    E   B7   A   E

_ I'm on _ my way, _ Great   God, I'm on my way. ____

_ I'm _ on _ my _ way, _ Great   God, I'm on my way. ____

I'll ask my brother to come and go with me,
I'll ask my brother to come and go with me,
I'll ask my brother

I'll ask my brother to come and go with me, (3)
I'm on my way, Great God, I'm on my way.

If he can't go, I'm gonna go anyhow, (3)
I'm on my way, Great God, I'm on my way

If you can't go, don't hinder me, (3)
I'm on my way, Great God, I'm on my way.

If you can't go let your children go, (3)
I'm on my way, Great God, I'm on my way.

I'm So Glad

Adaptation of traditional song

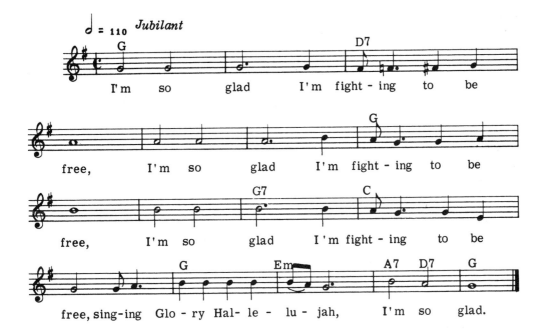

I'm so glad I'm fight-ing to be free, I'm so glad I'm fight-ing to be free, I'm so glad I'm fight-ing to be free, sing-ing Glo-ry Hal-le-lu-jah, I'm so glad.

I'm so glad I'm fighting to be free,
I'm so glad I'm fighting to be free,
I'm so glad I'm fighting to be free,
Singing Glory Hallelujah, I'm so glad.

I'm so glad jail can't stop us now, (3)
Singing Glory Hallelujah, I'm so glad.

I'm so glad we shall overcome, (3)
Singing Glory Hallelujah, I'm so glad.

I'm so glad our faith will see us
    through, (3)
Singing Glory Hallelujah, I'm so glad.

I'm so glad Mississippi's time has
    come, (3)
Singing Glory Hallelujah, I'm so glad.

I'm so glad I'm riding to be free, (3)
Singing Glory Hallelujah, I'm so glad.

Oh Freedom

Adaptation of traditional song by members of SNCC

"There is still, for me, no pathos quite like the pathos of those multi-colored, worn somehow triumphant and transfigured faces, speaking from the depths of a visible, tangible, continuing despair of the goodness of the Lord. I have never seen anything to equal the fire and excitement that sometimes, without warning, fill a church, causing the church, as Leadbelly and so many others have testified, to 'rock'."
— James Baldwin — "Letter from a Region in My Mind"

"I still hear the rhythm of the hoes hitting the red earth. I still hear the deep moaning hymns of the people in the white wooden churches beside the dusty roads of a Sunday morning. I still can taste the sweet corn bread I shared at table with a sharecropper and his family. Brown faces and worn shoes. Backs that bent under the sun all day were straight and tall each Night."

— Peggy Day

free ———————— and there'll be———
free. ———————

No segregation, no segregation, no
    segregation over me,
And before I'll be a slave, I'll be
    buried in my grave
And go home to my Lord and be free

No more weeping . . .

No more shooting . . .

No burning churches . .

No more jail house . . .

Oh, freedom . . .

No more Jim Crow . . .

No more Barnett . . .

No more Pritchett . . .

Over My Head

Traditional (African-American Spiritual)
Adapted by Bernice Johnson Reagon.

The old song said, "over my head I see trouble in the air." Bernice Johnson, one of the great song leaders in Albany, made this her song and substituted Freedom for trouble. She was expelled from Albany State College for her participation in the movement, went on to Spelman College and now travels with the Freedom Singers.

"Tears that had long since been clotted in dry throats gushed forth when another neighbor raised his hand at meeting to tell he'd been down to the court house to register and next week all his family was going to be there."

— Peggy Day

Sung very slowly & freely,
(without accompaniment)

O- ver my head _____ (2) I see I see
free-dom in the air, O- ver my head, ____ Oh, Lord, ____
vic-t'ry in the air,
____ I see free-dom in the air, O- ver my
head _____ I see free- dom in the air, There
must be a God _____ some - where.

Walkin' For Freedom
Just Like John

♩ = 152 CHORUS

I wan-na be read-y, I wan-na be read-y, — Lord, I wan-na be read-y,

walk-in' for free-dom a just a like John, Oh, —

just a like John, John, — he said that the jail was a

(Leader)

just a four square, — walk-in' for free-dom a

(response)

just a like John. And — we — de-clared that we'd

meet a him there, — Walk-in' for free-dom a just a like John. Oh, —

(Response)

VOTER REGISTRATION

Fayette County, Tennessee

Southwest Georgia

Mississippi Delta

Alabama

As this book is being compiled, students are working in rural areas around Albany, over in the Mississippi Delta and in other areas of the deep South trying to get people to cast off their fears, register and vote. As a result many of these students have had their lives threatened, suffered beatings and gunshot wounds, while local people who have responded have lost their jobs, been cut off relief, had their homes shot into and their churches burned. One man, Herbert Lee of Amite County, Mississippi, has been killed. A SNCC field secretary, James Travis, was shot and seriously wounded by three white men. In spite of the danger, students continue to work in these areas. All of these new events and the students' determination are reflected in the continually growing body of freedom songs.

The newest song "We'll Never Turn Back" commemorates the death of Herbert Lee:

We have hung our heads and cried
For those like Lee who died
Died for you and died for me
Died for the cause of equality
But we'll never turn back
Until we've all been freed.

One Man's Hands

Words: Alex Comfort   Music: Pete Seeger

"All our lives we've had to bow and scrape, laugh when there was nothing funny and scratch our heads and say 'yes sir.' We want to change that; we want to be men; that's what the power of the vote can do. . . . It's people like you, with faith in God, who are going to change this country. And we'll do it together."

— Charles Sherrod, SNCC worker in southwest Georgia, speaking at a mass meeting in 'terrible Terrell' County.

"The seed has been planted, the Freedom Seed. And these people are farmers and they know that for a crop to grow it's got to be watered and tended and pruned and worked over. They know seeds take time to sprout. They know that sometimes rain will flood a field and ruin a month's work in a cane field. They know it takes time and sweat and faith. And Freedom is the kind of seed that's old but must be planted anew each day."

— Peggy Day

One man's hands can't tear a pris-on down, _____ Two men's hands can't tear a pris-on down, _____ But if two and two and fif-ty make a mil-lion, _ we'll see that day come 'round, we'll see that day come 'round. _____

One man's feet can't walk across the
     South,
Two men's feet can't walk across the
     South,
But if two and two and fifty make a
     hundred,
We'll see that day come 'round,
We'll see that day come 'round.

One man's eyes can't see across the
     land . . .

One man's vote can't change the status
     quo . . .

One James Meredith can't integrate
     'Ole Miss' . . .

One Bob Moses can't integrate
     Mississippi . . .

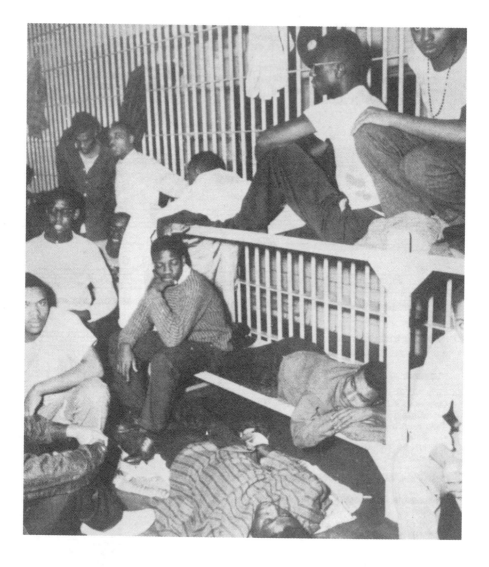

Woke Up This Morning
With My Mind on Freedom

'Reverend Osby of Aurora, Illinois, made up this revamp of an old gospel song ('I woke up this morning with my mind stayed on Jesus') in the Hinds County Jail during the Freedom Rides. It later spread to Albany and the surrounding communities. In Mississippi it went from the jails to McComb where one of the earliest voter campaigns began, and it is now sung all across the state.

120 students, marched out of the Burgland High School in protest over the murder of Herbert Lee, a voter registration worker, and the expulsion of their school-mate, Brenda Travis, who had participated in a sit-in at the local bus station.

"Early that Wednesday morning, October 4, 1961, I had arrived at the Negro Masonic lodge in McComb for a SNCC staff meeting. To my inquiry of 'How are you this morning?', Charles Sherrod, Bernard La Fayette, Chuck McDew and the other SNCC people answered in chorus, 'We woke up this morning with our minds stayed on Freedom!' They told me how Eugene Hurst, a Mississippi State Legislator had shot Herbert Lee and about the mass meeting held the night before where the high school students had declared their intention of demonstrating if Brenda Travis was not reinstated and if nothing was done about Lee's murder.

"That afternoon in a bare room over a grocery store that doubled as Masonic lodge and SNCC office, we huddled together near a window facing the school. As the singing of the students grew louder, the words changed from 'we'll walk hand in hand' to 'I woke up this morning with my mind stayed on freedom.' Soon we could hear the tramp of their feet and see their proud but grim smiles. As they swung around the corner of the concrete block building we joined them -- 'it ain't no harm to keep your mind stayed on freedom!' " -- Bob Zellner

mind ____ stayed ____ on free - dom, (Oh well I)

mind ____ stayed ____ on free - dom, Oh well I

woke up this morn - ing with my mind (my mind it was)

woke up this morn - ing with my mind, my mind it was

stayed ____ on free - dom, Hal - le - lu, hal - le - lu, hal - le -

stayed on free - dom Hal - le - lu, hal - le - lu, hal - le -

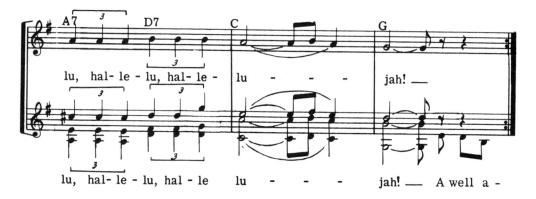

lu, hal - le - lu, hal - le - lu - - - jah! ____

lu, hal - le - lu, hal - le lu - - - jah! ____ A well a -

occasional variation:

Ain't no harm to keep your mind stayed
    on freedom,
Ain't no harm to keep your mind stayed
    on freedom,
Ain't no harm to keep your mind stayed
    on freedom,
Hallelu, hallelu, hallelu, hallelu,
    hallelujah!

Walkin' and talkin' with my mind stayed
    on freedom . . .

Singin' and prayin' with my mind stayed
    on freedom . . .

Doin' the twist with my mind stayed on
    freedom . . .

Get On Board, Little Children

Adaptation of traditional song by Sam Block & Willie
Peacock (SNCC)

Two SNCC workers in Mississippi revised this song:

"We were hungry one day and didn't
have anything to eat and didn't even
have a pair of shoes hardly, and we
went down and started hustling and a
fellow gave me a pair of shoes. Then
we had to ride a mule up there in Holly
Springs to get people to register.
Didn't even have transportation. But
we kept on begging for transportation.
Came up to Memphis and had to stay
five days and still didn't get a car.
But we're not worryin'. We ain't com-
plaining. We just go on and raise hell
all the time. We don't have to ride,
we can walk, anything, we don't care.

Ross Barnett talk all that stuff
about we ain't gonna do anything in
Mississippi, but he don't know. The
sheriff told Sam, 'I don't want to see
you down here no more.' Sam looked
at him and said, 'Well Sheriff, if you
don't want to see me, you better leave
town."

— Samuel Block and
Willie Peacock

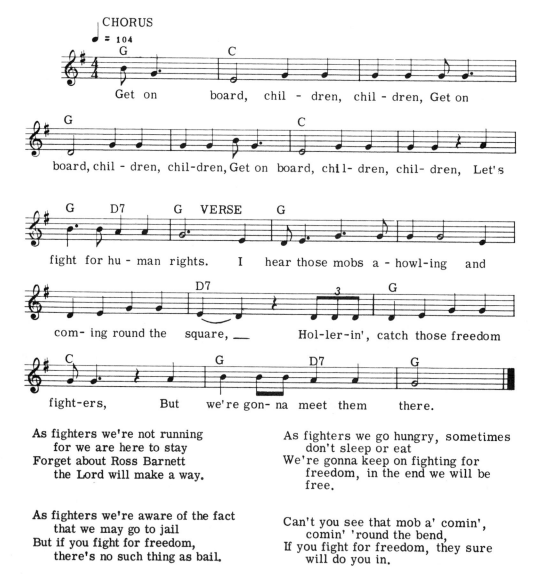

Get on board, chil - dren, chil - dren, Get on
board, chil - dren, chil-dren, Get on board, chil- dren, chil- dren, Let's
fight for hu - man rights. I hear those mobs a - howl-ing and
com- ing round the square, ___ Hol-ler-in', catch those freedom
fight-ers, But we're gon- na meet them there.

As fighters we're not running
   for we are here to stay
Forget about Ross Barnett
   the Lord will make a way.

As fighters we're aware of the fact
   that we may go to jail
But if you fight for freedom,
   there's no such thing as bail.

As fighters we go hungry, sometimes
   don't sleep or eat
We're gonna keep on fighting for
   freedom, in the end we will be
   free.

Can't you see that mob a' comin',
   comin' 'round the bend,
If you fight for freedom, they sure
   will do you in.

Come By Here

Words & music: Marvin V. Frey

"We are a little fed up with this voter registration business . . . we want our colored people to live like they've been living for the last hundred years — peaceful and happy."
> — Sheriff Z. T. Mathews, when he interrupted and broke up a mass meeting in Terrell County

"In the South, courage is a quiet thing. It may be born in a candle-lit farmhouse far back on a cornfield late one night over a pot of greens. Or one morning a man might wake up and decide to go down to the courthouse to register and because he doesn't have a car he might walk the 9 miles into town."
> — Peggy Day

Come by here, my Lord, Come by here, Come by here, my Lord, Come by

here, Come by here, my Lord, Come by here, Oh Lord, come by here.

Churches are burning Lord, come by here (3 times)
Oh Lord, come by here.

Somebody's shooting Lord, come by here . . .

Somebody's starving Lord, come by here . . .

We want justice Lord, come by here . . .

We want freedom Lord, come by here . . .

Fighting For My Rights

"I was expelled from my high school for speaking up for better facilities and more civil rights. The day after I was expelled, most of the students demonstrated in protest, and that night over 800 parents came out to a PTA meeting and signed a petition protesting my expulsion. When the administration refused to let me back in, the students and parents boycotted the school for over three months. During this time only approximately 150 out of 1300 students attended school and the county lost over $20,000. The white land-owners evicted some of the sharecropper parents and put so much pressure on the rest, the boycott was finally ended.

"After that I began helping the SNCC workers who had come to Lee County to work on voter registration. At first I drove them around and introduced them to people in the county, and later I helped canvas the area for potential voters. During this time I tried to register myself on five different occasions. I had just turned eighteen. But the county officials refused to let me.

"Soon our home was fired into and we had to get armed friends to help protect our house at night. This also happened to several others. Then Shady Grove Baptist Church was burned. We had held six or seven meetings there for people in the county interested in discussing voter registration and other problems." -- Charles Wingfield

Charles Neblett had the original idea of adapting Ray Charles' Lonely Avenue after his experiences in the Charleston, Mississippi jail. Charles Wingfield added several verses later as the song began obtaining widespread circulation.

You know I'm tired of se-gre-ga-tion and I want my e-qual rights; se-gre-ga-tion did me wrong, made me leave my hap-py home, That's why I'm fight-ing for my rights,— fight-ing for my rights, You know I'm fight-ing for my rights, (you know I'm) fight-ing for my rights.—

You know I'm tired of segregation and
   I want my equal rights
Segregation did me wrong, made me
   leave my happy home.

Chorus:
That's why I'm fighting for my rights,
   fighting for my rights
You know I'm fighting for my rights,
   fighting for my rights.

My mother, yeah, she told me
On her dying bed
Son if you don't get your freedom
You know I'd rather see you dead.

Well my father, yes, he told me
A long, long time ago
Son, if you don't fight for freedom
You'll be a slave forever more.

Well-a I want my freedom
And I want it now
And no matter what happens
I'm gonna fight on anyhow.

Well my cell it had two windows
But the sun could never come thru'
And I felt so sad and lonely
You know I didn't know what to do.

Well an old lady told me
And she was very brave
She said before she'll be a slave
She'd be buried in her grave.

Been Down Into the South

Adaptation of a traditional song by Bob Zellner (SNCC).

This old spiritual was first adapted by Bob Zellner, SNCC field secretary, in a car on the way back to Atlanta from Baton Rouge where he had been arrested, jailed and indicted for "criminal anarchy". Charles McDew, SNCC chairman, and also under indictment for the same charge was one of those singing in the car and helping improvise this new freedom song.

Later Bob introduced it to the Talladega student movement during their protest campaign against segregated public facilities. It immediately became one of the most popular songs at their mass meetings, demonstrations and jam sessions. Since then it has spread to other areas and taken on new verses.

I haven't been to heaven but I think I'm
right
Been down into the South
There's folk up there both black and
white
Been down into the South.

Chorus:
Hallelujah, freedom
Hallelujah, freedom
Hallelujah, freedom
Been down into the South.

I want to go to heaven but I want to go
   right,
Been down into the South,
I don't want to go without my civil
   rights.
Been down into the South. (Cho.)

Segregation is chilly and cold,
Chills my body but not my soul. (Cho.)

Freedom sounds so mighty sweet,
Soon one day we're gonna meet. (Cho.)

I been knockin' on doors and spreadin'
   the news,
And gettin' big holes in the bottom of
   my shoes. (Cho.)

Yes I've got big holes in the bottom of
   my shoes,
But this is one battle we can't lose.
   (Cho.)

If you don't think I've been through
   Hell,
Just follow me down to the Parchman
   jail. (Cho.)

You can talk about me just as much as
   you please,
Well the more you talk I'm gonna bend
   my knees. (Cho.)

The only thing that we did wrong,
Stayed in the wilderness a day too long.
   (Cho.)

The only thing that we did right
Was the day we started to fight. (Cho.)

We are fighting both black and white,
Fighting for our civil rights. (Cho.)

"On a Saturday afternoon in February, 1962, Chuck McDew and I went to visit Dion Diamond, a SNCC field secretary, who was confined in the East Baton Rouge Parish Jail, Louisiana.

"When told we could not visit Dion, we got permission to bring him some books and fruit. We returned with the articles and were promptly arrested for vagrancy and criminal anarchy, carrying a sentence of 10 years at hard labor, and placed under $7,000 bond apiece.

"I was cursed and shoved into an open cell block with 65 other white prisoners. The police brought papers to the other prisoners with stories saying that Chuck McDew, Negro, and Bob Zellner were subversive integrationists and were trying to overthrow the government of the state of Louisiana.

"They incited the other prisoners, most of them Southerners, to beat me up. For four days I faced men with sharpened spoons and razor blades who said they would eventually castrate me and 'pin me to my mattress.'

"Finally our lawyers forced the police to remove me from the open cell block. The police, announcing unceremoniously 'you goin' to the hole', pushed me into a 5' by 7' cell with a 5 inch square puncture in the steel door for ventilation.

"I didn't know that Chuck too was in solitary and I wondered where he was and how he was faring. Suddenly I heard his voice at my shoulder calling in a loud whisper, 'Bob, Bob, is that you?'

"I put my ear to a grate in the ceiling, then finally jumped down to the small vent in the door, realizing his voice was coming from there. There was Chuck's face reflected in a piece of metal on the stone wall across from my cell. He was in the cell next to me. 'Chuck, are you all right?' . . . 'Yes, you?' . . . 'Fine.'

"Then we sang. As the police pounded on the door threatening to whip us we sang, 'Woke Up This Morning With My Mind On Freedom.' Even after they turned the heaters on and blasted us with unbearable heat for seven days, we continued to sing — 'We'll walk hand in hand . . .' "

-- Bob Zellner

We'll Never Turn Back

Adaptation of a traditional song with new words & music by Bertha Gober (SNCC).

On September 25, 1962, Herbert Lee of Amite, Mississippi, was shot to death by State Representative Eugene Hurst. Students who were working then with SNCC's campaign to register Negro voters in Mississippi feel that Lee's death was a result of his having helped them meet local people and arrange gatherings. An economic squeeze was being put on Negroes involved in the voter campaign and Lee owed Hurst a sum of money. Eugene Hurst accosted Herbert Lee with a gun and the men argued. When it was over Lee was dead. An all white Coroner's jury ruled that the killing was in self defense and justifiable. A month later the Grand Jury refused to indict Hurst.

Bertha Gober wrote this song in commemoration of Herbert Lee.

turn back, No, we'll nev - er turn ___ back ___

(on last chorus)
to CODA

Un - til we've all ___ been freed and we have e -

2nd VERSE

qual- i - ty. ___ We have walked thru the shad-ows of death

we've had to walk all by our-selves. —

to CHORUS

3
We have served our time in jail
With no money for to go our bail. (Cho.)

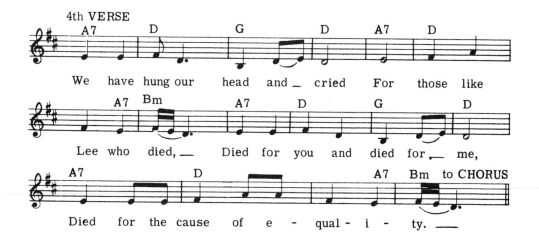

4th VERSE

We have hung our head and — cried For those like

Lee who died, — Died for you and died for — me,

Died for the cause of e - qual - i - ty. —

to CHORUS

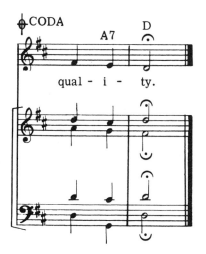

CODA

qual - i - ty.

Ballad of Herbert Lee

Based on accounts related to Bob Moses
by eye-witnesses at the scene of the
crime.
words: Ernie Marrs & Guy Carawan
tune: traditional (Irish)

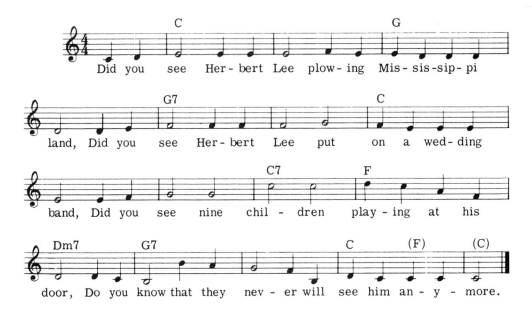

Did you see Herbert Lee plow-ing Mis-sis-sip-pi land, Did you see Her-bert Lee put on a wed-ding band, Did you see nine chil-dren play-ing at his door, Do you know that they nev-er will see him an-y-more.

Did you see Herbert Lee
  plowing Mississippi land?
Did you see Herbert Lee
  put on a wedding band?
Did you see nine children
  playing at his door?
Do you know that they never
  will see him anymore?

Did you see Herbert Lee
  help his people try to vote?
Did you see Herbert Lee
  damned for what he said and wrote?
Did you see the White Citizens
  Council meet in town?
Did you see Herbert Lee
  telling folks to stand their ground?

Did you see Herbert Lee
  haul his cotton to the gin?
Did you see him tailed
  by a local Congressman?
Did you see E. H. Hurst
  park behind him in that place?
Did you see E. H. Hurst
  poke a pistol in his face?

Did you see E. H. Hurst
  tell him "Get out on the ground"?
Did you see Lee say "First,
  you must put that pistol down"?
Did you see E. H. Hurst
  put his gun away once more?
Did you see Herbert Lee
  sliding out the furthest door?

Did you see E. H. Hurst
  come swiftly running 'round?
Did you see his gun
  out to shoot poor Herbert down?
Did you see Herbert Lee
  when he climbed down from his truck?
Did you see Herbert Lee
  when the white man's bullet struck?

Did you see him fall
  with empty hands outthrust?
Did you see Herbert Lee
  in the Mississippi dust?
Did you see him lay
  two hours in the sun?
Did you see no one dared
  to touch him -- no, not one?

Did you see, did you see
    how murder gets disguised?
Did you see, did you see
    a witness terrorized?
Did you see perjury
    done upon the witness stand?
It's a lie, Herbert Lee
    had no tire tool in his hand.

Did you see the witness ask
    Uncle Sam's protection there?
Did you see him reply,
    "I can't put guards everywhere"?
Did you see, did you see
    what a frightened witness saw?
Did you see, did you see
    a deputy break his jaw?

Did you see, did you see
    that no one went to jail?
Did you see an attempt made to
    straighten out the tale?
Will we see, will we see
    that story told again?
Will we see E. H. Hurst be
    judged by honest men?

Mrs. Lee, did you see
    a better life ahead?
Did you see it seem
    to die when Herbert did?
Did you see him fall for
    the cause of liberty?
Will you see someone else
    carry on for Herbert Lee?

The Hammer Song

Written by Pete Seeger and Lee Hays, this song was first introduced into the South at the singing sessions and song book of Highlander Folk School's Citizenship School classes by Julius Lester.

"OK. I have a plantation and don't try and register anybody on that plantation. I got a shotgun waiting for you."
— Ben Weed of Ruleville, Mississippi

With strong beat

If I had a ham-mer, —— I'd ham-mer in the morn-ing, — I'd ham-mer in the eve-ning —— all o-ver the land; I'd ham-mer at dan-ger, — I'd ham-mer out a warn-ing, — I'd ham-mer out love be-tween all of my broth-er, (my broth-ers and my sis-ters) All —— o-ver this land. ——

If I had a bell, I'd ring it in the morning,
I'd ring it in the evening all over this land,
I'd ring out danger, I'd ring out a warning,
I'd ring out love between my brothers and my sisters,
All over this land.

If I had a song, I'd sing it in the morning, etc . . .

Well I've got a hammer and I've got a bell
And I've got a song to sing all over this land,
It's the hammer of justice, it's the bell of freedom,
It's the song about love between my brothers and my sisters,
All over this land.

98

GREENWOOD, BIRMINGHAM...

Since the first tentative completion of this book, many additional areas have erupted. There will certainly be more. After the long tedious months of voter registration work in Mississippi, Greenwood became the first major breakthrough. In spite of the attacks by policemen and police dogs, over three thousand people have now walked down to attempt registration there. (Only thirty have been registered, but the fact that so many have been willing to put aside their fear and make the attempt is vitally important.)

The Birmingham demonstrations represented a turning point for the country. Never before had such numbers gone to jail. Over 3,000 Birmingham Negroes were jailed. Following the news of police brutality, the use of dogs and fire hoses and the jailing of over 2,000 children and high school students, demonstrations began to flare all across the country, north and south. Jackson, Mississippi; Gadsden, Alabama; Danville, Virginia; Cambridge, Maryland; Detroit, Los Angeles, New York and numerous other cities in the U.S. were faced with thousands of Negroes making their grievances known. According to CORE statistics, over 12,500 civil rights demonstrators were arrested in the three months following Birmingham.

"No state in the South has remained untouched this year, and in an amazing number of cities -- Nashville, Knoxville, Durham, Charlotte, to mention only a few -- dramatic victories in the opening of public accomodations have been won very quickly.

In the early days of the Sit-In Movement it was mostly college students involved; today the movement cuts across all age lines -- from small school children to grandparents -- and across all class lines. Then the conflagration was basically in the South and Northerners helped only by sending contributions; today people in the North are facing up to de facto segregation at home and are borrowing from the South the technique of direct action to meet it.

More important, the goals today are quite different. Then the target of the students was mainly the lunch counters. Today there is scarcely a city in the South where the announced goal of the integration movement is less than an "open city" -- a phrase that has come to mean the complete erasure of the color line in all facilities serving the public.

And significantly, more and more, along with demands for opened public accommodations are being coupled demands for equal job opportunities." The Southern Patriot, June, 1963.

With the terrific upsurge in protest came violence and death. Bill Moore was shot to death on a highway in Alabama. Medgar Evers was murdered when he came home from a strategy-planning meeting in Jackson, Mississippi. A church in Birmingham was bombed and four young Negro girls were killed. In the aftermath policemen killed a Negro boy throwing rocks at cars of white people. (This was the sixth time that Negroes had been bombed in Birmingham since the demonstrations started there. Seven Negroes have been killed as a result of the bombings and the riots afterwards.)

As a result of the growing racial pressure and potential violence in the U.S. since the Birmingham demonstrations, the President and Federal Government finally gave some special attention to the situation. New Civil Rights legislation is before the Congress now.

On August 28th, more than 200,000 Negroes and whites from across the nation, representing all the major civil rights organizations, marched on Washington D. C., expressing in a quiet, orderly and meaningful fashion their demands for action now. The official theme song of the march was We Shall Overcome.

Following are a few examples of new songs that have grown out of the most recent period in the civil rights struggle. They are beginning to take their place in the body of already well-established freedom songs.

Guide My Feet While I Run This Race

Adaptation of traditional song by members of SNCC

"I received a call from an individual who identified himself as speaking for the White Citizens Council. He told me, 'If you take anybody else up to register, you'll never leave Greenwood alive.' I get such calls with some frequency."

Sam Block in a routine report to the SNCC office.

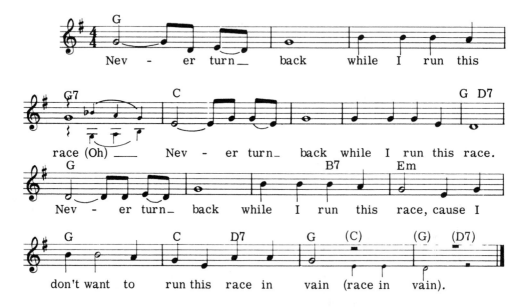

Nev - er turn back while I run this race (Oh) Nev - er turn back while I run this race. Nev - er turn back while I run this race, cause I don't want to run this race in vain (race in vain).

Never turn back, while I run this
race (3 times)
'Cause I don't want to run this race
in vain.

Guide my feet while I run this race
(3 times)
'Cause I don't want to run this race
in vain.

Guide my heart. . . . .

Guide my tongue. . . . .

Guide my vote. . . . .

Guide my mind. . . . .

Bull Connor's Jail

tune: "Down in the Valley"
"Birmingham Jail"
words: Ernie Marrs

Guy & Candie Carawan were arrested entering New Pilgrim Baptist Church where they had been invited to sing and record a mass meeting. They spent the next 18 hours in the white men's and women's drunk tanks at the City Jail. Police officers and jail guards tried to incite prisoners against them saying that they were freedom riders. When those at the mass meeting heard of their arrest, over 1,000 marched to a park near the jail where they serenaded the prisoners with freedom songs. From a third-floor cell Candie was able to see fire trucks and hoses being unrolled as the crowd arrived. On his stone bench in the basement, Guy could hear the dogs barking outside. Through the night, they could hear freedom songs being sung by the Negro prisoners in the distance.

Down in Alabama, in the land of Jim
  Crow,
There is a place where lots of folks
  go.

    CHORUS: Birmingham jailhouse,
      Birmingham jail;
      Waiting for freedom
      In Bull Connor's jail.

Three thousand prisoners, more
  coming on;
Even little children are singing this
  song.

Bull Connor tells us, "Don't raise a
  squawk,
You need a permit even to walk."

Went to the church house, to sing
  and to pray;
Started downtown and they hauled us
  away.

Pushed by policemen, herded like
  hogs -
Some got the fire hose, some got
  the dogs.

Crammed in like sardines in Bull
  Connor's can,
Some can lay down, but others must
  stand.

Here comes a cockroach, big as a
  whale;
He feels at home in Bull Connor's
  jail.

Iron bars around me, cold walls so
  strong;
They hold my body, the world hears
  my song.

Let's spread the story, let's tell the
  tale,
Let's tell the world of Bull Connor's
  jail.

Ballad For Bill Moore

tune: "You've Got To Walk That
Lonesome Valley"
words: Don West

On April 24, 1963, a Baltimore post-man, CORE member William L. Moore, was shot from behind on U. S. Highway 11 near Gadsden, Alabama. Moore, a native Mississippian, was journeying to present his personal plea for civil rights to Governor Ross Barnett.

Members of SNCC and CORE who later decided to carry through his pilgrim-age to Jackson were pelted with rocks and eggs by mobs of hoodlums and then arrested at the Alabama state line by policemen using electric prod poles to force the demonstrators into patrol cars.

CHORUS
Oh, Bill Moore walked that lone - some high - way, He dared to walk there by him - self, None of us here were walk - ing with him, He walked that high-way by him - self.

VERSE
Yes, he walked to A - la - ba - ma, He walked that road for you and me, In his life there was the pur - pose, That black and white might both be free.

He walked for peace, he walked for
  freedom,
He walked for truth, he walked for
  right
End segregation in this country
Eat at joe's both black and white. (Cho.)

The lyncher's bullets know no color
As they come whining thru the night,
They've brought death to many a Negro
And William Moore whose skin was
  white.

They shot him down in cold blood
  murder
Two bullet holes were in his head,
His body lay upon the road-way
Where lynchers left him cold and dead.
  (Cho.)

Each man must walk his lonesome
  highway
Each must decide it for himself,
No one else can do that for you,
You've got to walk there by yourself!

Some day we'll all walk there together
And we'll knock on Freedom's door
And if they ask, who was it sent you,
We'll say a man nar ' William Moore.

He walked for peace, he walked for
  freedom
He walked for truth, he walked for
  right,
End segregation in this country
Eat at Joe's, both black and white.

Hard Travelin'

Words & music: Woody Guthrie   New verses: Guy Carawan

I've been doing some hard travelin'
   I thought you knowed,
I've been doing some hard travelin'
   Way down the road,
Well if you don't think I've been
   through hell
Just follow me down to the Greenwood
   jail
      I've been havin' some hard
         travelin', Lord.

I've been walkin' the streets of
   Ruleville
   I thought you knowed,
I've been walkin' the streets of
   Ruleville
   Way down the road,
I've been knockin' on doors and
   spreadin' the news
And wearin' big holes in the bottom
   of my shoes
      I've been havin' some hard
         canvassing, Lord.

I've been layin' in a hard-rock jail
   I thought you knowed,
I've been layin' out ninety days
   Way down the road,

That mean old judge he said to me
It's ninety days for vagrancy,
      Well I've been havin' some hard
         travelin', Lord.

I've been walkin' the streets of
   Greenwood
   I thought you knowed,
I've been walkin' the streets of
   Greenwood
   Way down the road,
Guns a-blastin', bullets a-flyin'
Poor Jimmy Travis almost dyin'
      He's been havin' some hard
         travelin', Lord.

I've been havin' some hard travelin'
   I thought you knowed,
I've been working in Holly Springs
   Way down the road,
Got my hand on the freedom plow
I wouldn't take nothin' for my journey
   now
      Well I've been havin' some hard
         travelin', Lord.

Ninety-Nine and a Half Won't Do

This is one of the many modern gospel songs that the choir of the Birmingham Movement has adapted to fit the spirit of the Southern freedom struggle. The variety of singing to be heard at mass meetings in Birmingham probably hasn't been matched in any other movement in the South. Starting off with an old time prayer service in which the older people sing and line out the old time spirituals and "Dr. Watts" hymns in a style which goes back to slavery days, the meetings are then turned over to the songs of the movement's sixty voice gospel choir accompanied by the organ playing of its leader. After the church has rocked and spirits are jubilant, it is time to hear from their leader, Reverend Fred Shuttleworth. Later the congregation will join the young people in singing some of the new freedom songs that are being sung in other parts of the South.

Keep Your Eyes on the Prize

Music: traditional ("Keep Your Hand on the Plow")
Words Adapted by Alice Wine & the Civil Rights Movement
© 1963, 1965 Alice Wine. All Rights Reserved. Used by Permission.

This is a song that has been through every chapter of the movement. The words "keep your eyes on the prize" (replacing the more common "keep your hand on the plow") came from Alice Wine, one of the first proud products of voter education schools -- on Johns Island, South Carolina in 1956.

The song had meaning for the sit-in students who were the first to be 'bound in jail' for long periods of time. It went with the Freedom Riders to Jackson and into Parchman, and then on to Albany and all of the many other areas of struggle.

Paul and Silas begin to shout, the jail door opened and they walked on out.
Keep your eyes on the prize, hold on.

Freedom's name is mighty sweet, soon one day we're gonna meet.

Got my hand on the Gospel plow, I wouldn't take nothing for my journey now.

The only chain that a man can stand, is that chain of hand in hand.

The only thing we did wrong, stayed in the wilderness a day too long.

But the one thing we did right, was the day we started to fight.

We're gonna board that big Greyhound, carryin' love from town to town.

We're gonna ride for civil rights, we're gonna ride both black and white.

We've met jail and violence too, but God's love has seen us through.

Haven't been to heaven but I've been told, streets up there are paved with gold.

FREEDOM IS A CONSTANT STRUGGLE
Songs of the Freedom Movement

COMPILED AND EDITED BY GUY AND CANDIE CARAWAN

WITH DOCUMENTARY PHOTOGRAPHS / MUSIC TRANSCRIPTIONS BY ETHEL RAIM

TABLE OF CONTENTS
Freedom Is A Constant Struggle

I GOT ON MY TRAVELLING SHOES
Birmingham AL, St. Augustine FL, Danville VA, Atlanta GA, Americus GA (1963-64) 116

Travelling Shoes 118
Great Day For Me 121
Birmingham Sunday 122
We've Got A Job 126
We're Gonna March in St. Augustine 128
I Love Everybody 131
Wade In The Water 132
Legend of Danville 134
Demonstrating G.I. 136
Oginga Odinga 138
Prophecy of a SNCC Field Secretary 142
You Should Have Been There 148
I Ain't Scared A' Your Jail 150
Nothing But A Soldier 152
Go Ahead 154
Up Over My Head *(Betty Mae Fikes)* 156

FREEDOM IS A CONSTANT STRUGGLE
Mississippi Project (Summer 1964) 160

Why Was The Darkie Born? 162
Freedom Train A' Comin' 166
Father's Grave 176
I Want My Freedom 181
It Isn't Nice 182
Mississippi Goddam 188
Freedom Is A Constant Struggle 196
We Got A Thing Going On 200
Go Tell It On The Mountain 204
Carry It On 208

I BEEN IN THE STORM SO LONG
The Return to Afro-American Roots 211

Throw Me Anywhere, Lord 217
Juba 218
Give Me The Gourd to Drink Water 220
Bullyin' Jack-A-Diamonds 223
Go Down Old Hannah 224
Delta Blues 228
Bourgeois Blues 230
Down On Me 235
I Been In The Storm So Long 236
I'll Be All Right 238
I Will Overcome 239

OH, WALLACE, YOU NEVER CAN JAIL US ALL
Selma, Alabama (1963-65) 242

This May Be The Last Time 252
Berlin Wall 254
Do What The Spirit Say Do 257
Right! Right! 259
Which Side Are You On? *(Len Chandler)* 260
Another Day's Journey 262
Oh, Wallace (You Never Can Jail Us All) 264
Murder On The Road In Alabama 268

WE GOT THE WHOLE WORLD SHAKIN'
Chicago and the North (1966-68) 272

I Don't Want To Be Lost In The Slums 279
Lead Poison On The Wall 280
Rent Strike Blues 282
Burn, Baby, Burn 284
People Get Ready 288
Never Too Much Love 290
Gonna Be A Meetin' Over Yonder 292
Freedom Now 296
We Got The Whole World Shakin' 300
Move On Over 307
Keep On Pushing 308

INTRODUCTION (From the 1968 edition)

"No more long prayers, no more Freedom songs, no more dreams – let's go for power."
— Stokely Carmichael, 1966

Here is a book of Freedom songs – songs that have evolved since the 1963 March on Washington. Already many of them seem outdated in light of the new mood within the Civil Rights Movement. The days of singing, "We love everybody... we love George Wallace" have passed. Many battle-scarred veterans of the last six years can no longer stand with arms crossed and sing with great hope and expectation that "the truth will make us free."

Since 1960 singing has been important to the movement. Every new chapter of the struggle produced its own songs. Birmingham, St. Augustine, Danville, Atlanta, Americus and elsewhere – campaign after campaign carried on the traditions of a singing movement. New songs were written; old ones adapted.

The 1964 Mississippi Summer Project left behind its songs, more diversified because of the participation of a thousand outsiders including northern songwriters. The Selma March in the spring of 1965 brought attention to a growing movement in the black belt of Alabama. The fifty-mile march was very conducive to the spontaneous improvisation of verse after verse after verse. Many songs got started there and carried elsewhere by the 40,000 marchers across the country. The march ended in front of the state capitol in Montgomery in a powerful show of "Black and white together..." singing "...We shall overcome." This will surely go down as a turning point – perhaps the last time that such a scene will be witnessed in this country for some time to come.

In 1966 there would be another march which, by its end, was almost all Negro and ringing with a new cry – "Black Power!" The Mississippi March began after the shooting of James Meredith and soon became a walking forum for Negro leaders discussing the merits of an all-black movement. There was dissension and argument, but it was clear to everyone that it was a time of change. At least two new songs expressing the new mood were heard – Len Chandler's angry "Move On Over or We'll Move On Over You" and Jimmy Collier's "Burn, Baby, Burn." "Burn, Baby, Burn" emerged when the Civil Rights Movement went north. Jimmy Collier, a young songwriter and organizer with Dr. King's End the Slum campaign in Chicago, wrote it in response to the Watts riots. A number of other new songs expressive of northern ghetto life have come out of the Chicago Movement. Many of them are based on rock & roll and rhythm & blues rather than spiritual and gospel songs. It should be noted that Dr. King and his co-workers are trying to keep their movement nonviolent and so far most of these new songs are in this vein. (But they are having a hard time convincing many ghetto dwellers who agree with a veteran of Watts when he declares, "Folk singing is out...karate is in.")

An important part of the new mood within the movement is a proud embracing of American folk heritage and its earlier African roots. There have been a number of festivals and conferences exploring this much neglected heritage. The excitement this has generated is spreading and is reflected in such diverse things as clothing, natural hairstyles, a new interest in folk ways and a respect for the folk qualities of a great leader like Mrs. Fannie Lou Hamer. Included in this development is a growing awareness and appreciation of Negro folk music. That is why we have included a chapter on the roots – old spirituals, children's songs, worksongs and blues – songs that have sung of freedom and protested in their own way, some of them since slavery times.

Since 1960 there have been tremendous changes in the Civil Rights Movement. The veterans of those six years have experienced disillusionment and growth. With the new demands of Black Power they are trying to grapple with more realistic ways to change our society.

Just what forms of expression, musical or otherwise, will accompany these new developments must be left to some future book.

— Guy and Candie Carawan

I GOT ON MY
TRAVELLING SHOES

Birmingham

St. Augustine

Danville

Atlanta

Americus

and elsewhere

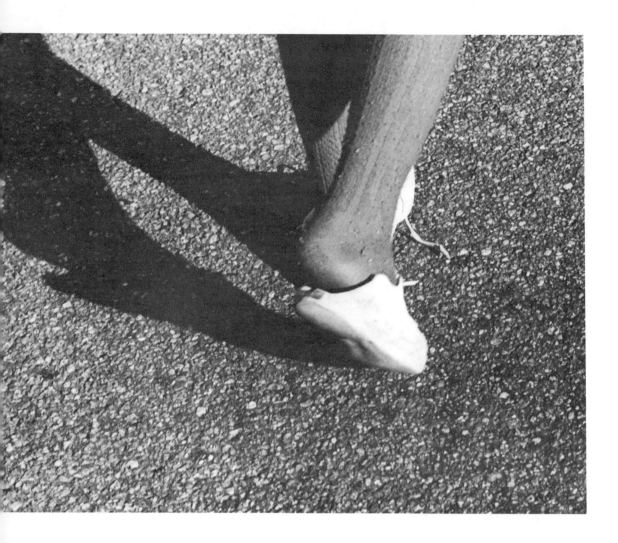

Travelling Shoes

Adaptation of spiritual Birmingham choir

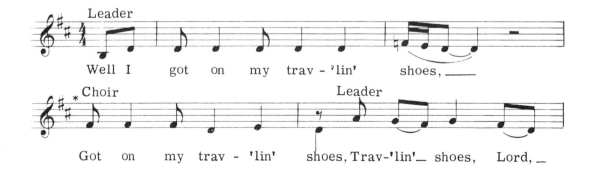

Leader

Well I got on my trav - 'lin' shoes, _____

Choir *

Got on my trav - 'lin' shoes, Trav-'lin'_ shoes, Lord, _

Leader

* Almost all the F♯ s are sung between F and F♯.

CHOIR

Got on my travellin' shoes (2x)
Got on my travellin' shoes (2x)
Got on my travellin' shoes (2x)
Got on my travellin' shoes (2x)
Got on my travellin' shoes (2x)
Got on my travellin' shoes (2x)

LEAD

Well I got on my travellin' shoes
I been travellin', Lord
Travellin' for freedom now
Fightin' for justice now
Don't you worry now
Travellin' shoes on

Birmingham, Alabama, 1963, became a major turning point in the civil rights movement. Thousands of local citizens, facing high pressure fire hoses and snarling police dogs, demonstrated. Over 3400 people, including 2000 students, went to jail. Developments in Birmingham triggered demonstrations in cities across the nation, creating the pressure which eventually produced the 1964 civil rights bill.

Great Day For Me

Adaptation of gospel song Birmingham choir

The sixty-voice Birmingham Movement gospel choir rocked mass meetings, making spirits jubilant, night after night for nearly three months.

Great day for me, great day for me, I am so hap-py, I want to be free, since Je-sus came to Bir-ming-ham, I'm hap-py as — can be, oh, ———— great day for me.

	LEAD	CHOIR
Great day for me, great day for me,	Great day for me	Great day for me
I'm so happy, I want to be free	Oh yes it is	Great day for me
Since Jesus came to Birmingham	I am so happy	I'm so happy
I'm happy as can be,	I'm going to be	I'm going to be
Oh...oh, great day for me.	free	free
		Since Jesus came to Birmingham
	Oh	I'm happy as can be
	Oh yes	Oh...oh, great day for me.

Birmingham Sunday

Words: Richard Fariña
Music: traditional ("I Loved a Lass")
© 1964 Vogue Music
c/o Welk Music Group, Santa Monica CA 90401.
All Rights Reserved. Used by Permission.

The accomplishments of Birmingham have not been gained without great pain.

"On Sunday morning, September 15, 1963, Claude Wesley stood chatting with the attendant who was filling his car's gas tank at a service station two blocks from the 16th Street Baptist Church. All at once the whole morning exploded. Hurled by the force of ten or fifteen sticks of dynamite, rocks and glass crashed like shells through the trees, and Wesley, fighting to deny himself what he knew had happened, raced toward the screams which were rising from the church.

'... Love your enemies, bless them that curse you, do good to them that hate you, and pray for them which despitefully use you, and persecute you' was the text for that morning.

As the bomb detonated and rafters buckled, the teacher shreiked, "Lie on the floor! Lie on the floor!' Even as she screamed, the face of Jesus in the church's prized stained-glass window shattered into fragments. "

Four young girls, including Claude Wesley's daughter, were dead.

Jack Mendelsohn, The Martyrs

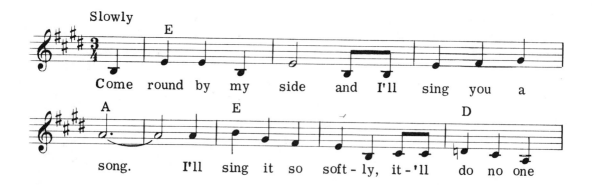

Slowly

Come round by my side and I'll sing you a song. I'll sing it so soft-ly, it-'ll do no one

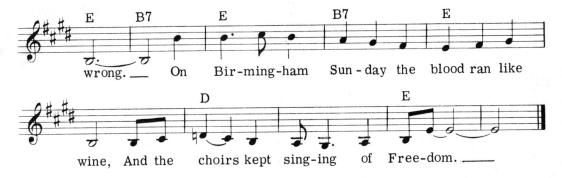

wrong. ___ On Bir-ming-ham Sun-day the blood ran like wine, And the choirs kept sing-ing of Free-dom. ___

Come round by my side and I'll sing you a song.
I'll sing it so softly, it'll do no one wrong.
On Birmingham Sunday the blood ran like wine,
And the choirs kept singing of Freedom.

That cold autumn morning no eyes saw the sun,
And Addie Mae Collins, her number was one.
At an old Baptist church there was no need to run.
And the choirs kept singing of Freedom.

The clouds they were grey and the autumn winds blew,
And Denise McNair brought the number to two.
The falcon of death was a creature they knew,
And the choirs kept singing of Freedom.

The church it was crowded, but no one could see
That Cynthia Wesley's dark number was three.
Her prayers and her feelings would shame you and me.
And the choirs kept singing of Freedom.

Young Carol Robertson entered the door
And the number her killers had given was four.
She asked for a blessing but asked for no more,
And the choirs kept singing of Freedom.

On Birmingham Sunday a noise shook the ground.
And people all over the earth turned around.
For no one recalled a more cowardly sound.
And the choirs kept singing of Freedom.

The men in the forest they once asked of me,
How many black berries grew in the Blue Sea.
And I asked them right back with a tear in my eye.
How many dark ships in the forest?

The Sunday has come and the Sunday has gone.
And I can't do much more than to sing you a song.
I'll sing it so softly, It'll do no one wrong.
And the choirs keep singing of Freedom.

We've Got A Job

Music and words:
Carlton Reese & B'ham choir

In 1966, the issue in Birmingham was voting. The demand was that registration be conducted in neighborhoods where Negroes live, and at night instead of only at the courthouse at hours inconvenient to working people. "We want the Courthouse brought out to the people", said Fred Shuttlesworth. As a result of many marches, federal registrars have now been sent to Birmingham. It is the first time they have been sent to an urban area where the Negro vote will have real power.

This is another of the freedom gospel songs of the Birmingham Movement Choir written by its organist-director, Carlton Reese.

I've got a job, I've got a job, and I want you to know, you've got a job, all of God's chil-dren, all of God's chil-dren, sure - ly, sure-ly got a job, we've got a job, — we've got a job to do, — we can't get free-dom 'til we get through, car-ryin' the cross of our Lord.

We are fight-ing for free - dom, come on, you

might not hear us   free - dom.   free -
dom The Con -sti -tu -tion of the U -nit -ed States
says _____ that we're due free--dom, freedom, freedom, freedom

LEAD

I've got a job
And I want you to know
All of God's children
Surely
We've got a job
We can't get freedom 'til we get through
Carrying' the cross of our Lord.

Talk to Bull Conner...
etc....

Talk to Mr. Wallace...
etc...

We are fighting for
Come on, you might not hear us
One time for Bull Conner
One time for Mayor Boutwell
One time for Gov. Wallace
One time for the city jail
One time for the city hall

The Consitution of the United States, says
That we're due freedom
                 freedom
                 justice
                 yes, Lord
                 freedom
We've got a job
We can't get freedom 'til we get through
Carrying the cross of our Lord.

CHOIR

I've got a job
You've got a job
All of God's children
Surely got a job
We've got a job to do

I've got a job
etc...

I've got a job...
etc...

Freedom
Freedom
Freedom
Freedom
Freedom
Freedom
Freedom

freedom
freedom (8x)
justice (4x)
yes, Lord (4x)
freedom (4x)
We've got a job to do

"St. Augustine was the South's last great demonstration campaign against legally supported segregation of public accommodations, the struggle continuing right up to signing of the civil rights law, as though to illustrate daily the desperate need for the law."

Pat Watters, New South

We're Gonna March In St. Augustine Tonight, My Lord

Adaption of spiritual - SCLC

"This was about the roughest city we've had -- forty-five straight nights of beatings and intimidation. In church every night we'd see people sitting there with bandages on. Some would sit with shotguns between their legs. We marched regularly at night. We kept being ordered not to march especially at night because it was so dangerous. We sang every night before we went out to get up our courage. The Klan was always waiting for us -- these folk with the chains and bricks and things -- Hoss Manucy and his gang. After we were attacked we'd come back to the church, and somehow always we'd come back bleeding, singing 'I love everybody..,' It was hard."

Dorothy Cotton - SCLC

We're gon - na march in St. Au - gus -tine tonight, my Lord, we're gon - na march in St. Au - gus -tine tonight, my Lord,— we're get-ting read - y, get-ting read-y for the

free-dom __ day, my Lord, __ my Lord. __ Are you

read - y for your free-dom? Oh, yes. __ Are you

read - y for the jour -ney? __ Oh yes. __ Do you

want your free - dom? __ Oh yes. __ We're gon - na

march in St. Au -gus-tine to - night, my Lord. __

CHORUS
We're gonna march in St. Augustine tonight, my Lord,
We're gonna march in St. Augustine tonight, my Lord,
We're getting ready, getting ready for the freedom day,
My Lord, my Lord.

Are you ready for your freedom?   Oh yes
Are you ready for the journey?   Oh yes
Do you want your freedom?   Oh yes
We're gonna march in St. Augustine tonight, my Lord.

CHORUS
We're gonna march...etc.

Are you ready, my sister?   Oh yes
Are you ready for the journey?   Oh yes
Do you want your freedom?   Oh yes
We're gonna march in St. Augustine tonight, my Lord.

"On two of St. Augustine's murky nights, after state troopers in large numbers had been called in against beatings, brick and acid throwing and other violence against non-violent demonstrations, white people bearing anti-Negro signs, led by racists, marched in a demonstration procession of their own through the main Negro neighborhood of the city. The troopers, in a line longer than the procession of 170, walked beside them to protect them, as they had also done for the Negroes. The white marchers included persons recognizable as members of the mob which had waited nightly to shout at and attack the Negro demonstrators. There were also children and women. Two boys, the age for Boy Scout hikes, shambled along, side by side, eyes excited.

When this strange procession, with the armed troopers flashing lights to both sides, their police dogs barking, reached the entrance to the Negro neighborhood, a sign greeted them: 'Welcome. Peace and brotherhood to you.'

On the second night, when the procession filed into the same street, it was lined on both sides by Negroes. Some held signs: 'I am an American'... 'Equality for all in '64'... They extended the length of the street, a good three blocks, outnumbering the white marchers probably three to one. They were still, almost motionless. And as the procession of whites, with Confederate flags and big American flag, and their own signs -- 'Kill the Civil Rights Bill'.. 'Put George Wallace on the Supreme Court' ... 'Don't Tread on Me' ... went by, the Negroes sang their song: 'I Love Everybody'.

Slowly, mournfully, softly, along the whole street, as the silent procession went by, they sang. An old Negro man and woman stood, arm in arm, staring at the white procession with eyes of loathing pain. 'I love everybody in my heart'... they sang. A second floor porch over a store was filled with Negroes, staring down, singing. 'Look up that nigger's dress,' one in the march said. Others shushed him. The song continued:

' I love everybody, I love everybody, I love everybody in my heart...You can't make me doubt Him, you can't make me doubt Him, You can't make me doubt Him in my heart.' "

Pat Watters, <u>New South</u>

130

I Love Everybody

Adaption of spiritual - SCLC

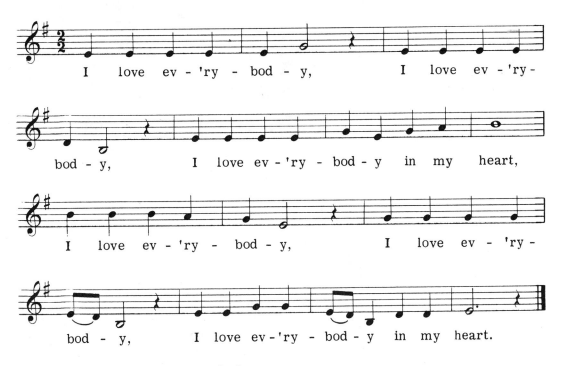

I love ev - 'ry - bod - y, I love ev - 'ry-

bod - y, I love ev - 'ry - bod - y in my heart,

I love ev - 'ry - bod - y, I love ev - 'ry-

bod - y, I love ev - 'ry - bod - y in my heart.

I love everybody, I love everybody,
 I love everybody in my heart,
You can't make me doubt Him,
 You can't make me doubt Him,
 You can't make me doubt Him in my heart.
The Klan can't make me doubt Him...

I feel the fire burning....

I know freedom is a-comin'...

I love Hoss Manucy...

"Then somebody would always stop, because it was hard to sing 'I love Hoss Manucy' when he'd just beat us up, to say a little bit about what love really was. He's still a person with some degree of dignity in the sight of God, and we don't have to like him, but we have to love him. He's been damaged too. So we sing it, and the more we sing it, the more we grow in ability to love people who mistreat us so bad."

Dorothy Cotton - SCLC

Wade In The Water

Traditional spiritual

"I remember the wade-ins because the bump hasn't gone off my jaw yet. We had taken a lot of kids down to the beach, not really realizing it was gonna be so bad. As I approached the water I could see it was tense -- all these policemen congregated there there and five or six feet away a group of hoodlums. They started yelling obscenities at us, but we went on -- myself and a group of teen-age girls. We were afraid but we felt we just had to go on.

We stood at the edge of the water for awhile and it was quiet -- an awful kind of quiet. Then two or three of the fellows would run and charge the group -- not hitting or anything, but just running into the group. The girls would just step aside. I thought they would leave us alone, so I encouraged the girls to go ahead and swim. Some fellows who were working with the movement, larger fellows, were out there; but somehow they picked on the group of girls.

Finally they really charged. It was obvious they felt they just couldn't take it anymore -- our being there. They knocked those little girls like they were men. One girl got a broken nose, and there were messed up eyes and faces.

There was a white fellow back on the beach saying to the policemen, 'you're supposed to protect them. Why don't you protect them?' And it was so obvious that they weren't there to protect us, but that they were friends of the hoodlums.

After the beating we went away. We sang, "Wade in the Water' and decided to go back another day. "

Dorothy Cotton - SCLC

Chorus

Wade in the wa - ter, wade in the

wa - ter, chil - dren, wade in the wa - ter,

Verse

God's gon - na trou - ble — the wa - ter. Well

Jor - dan Riv - er is chill - y and cold, —

God's gon - na trou - ble — the wa - ter, Well it

chills my bod - y but not my soul, —

God's gon - na trou - ble the wa - ter.

Wade in the water, wade in the water, children,
Wade in the water, God's gonna trouble the water.

Jordan River is chilly and cold, God's gonna trouble the water.
It chills my body, but not my soul, God's gonna trouble the water.

Tell me who's that comin' all dressed in white...
Well it looks like children fighting for their rights...

Tell me who's that coming all dressed in red...
Well it looks like children Martin Luther King led...

Wade in the water...

DANVILLE

Danville, Virginia, erupted into racial turmoil in late May, 1963, and ran a close race with Birmingham for top honors in police brutality. The issues were segregated public facilities, discrimination in employment, schools which were integrated in a token manner, and poor conditions generally in the Negro neighborhoods.

There were marches of protest almost every day from May 31 to June 5, culminating finally in the demonstrators being rushed and brutally beaten by policemen.

Legend Of Danville

Words & music: Matthew Jones

In Dan - ville on June the tenth __ in the year of six - ty - three, From Bi-ble - way Church __ to the court - house __ Some peo - ple marched to be free. __ Move on, __ Move on, __ Move on with the Free - dom __ fight. Move __ on, __ Move __ on, __ We're fight - ing for e - qual

Interlude after chorus of 6th verse

rights. Don't you stum-ble, bro - ther, don't you fal - ter, Oh moth - er, don't you _ weep, _ _ We're climb - ing up _ to our Free-dom _ _ al - though the road _ is _ steep. (To Cho.)

In Danville on June the tenth
In the year of sixty-three,
From Bibleway Church to the court-
    house
Some people marched to be free.

CHORUS: (after each verse)
Move on, move on, move on with the
    freedom fight.
Move on, move on, we're fighting for
    equal rights.

The night was dark and the journey
    long
As they marched two abreast
But with the spirit of freedom's song
They didn't need no rest.

As they fell down on their knees
Led by Reverend McGhee
He looked up and cried, 'Lord,
    please
We want to be free. '

They heard the voice of Chief
    McCann
As it cut across the prayer,
I'll never forget those violent words,
'Nigger, get out of here!'

And as they heard those brutal words
They didn't turn around
And the water from the fire hose
Knocked them to the ground.

And as they fell down on the ground
They were hit with the billy sticks
I'll never forget that terrible sound
As the people's heads did split.

CHORUS, and interlude:
Don't you stumble brother, don't you
    falter,
Oh mother, don't you weep,
We're climbing up to our freedom
Although the road is steep.

On June 13th we marched again
They used the tear gas bombs
The grand jury indicted us
On five thousand dollar bond.

In Danville town's corrupted courts
We got no justice done.
We were found guilty before the trial
And the judge he wore a gun.

Demonstrating G.I.

Words & music: Matthew Jones
© 1963, 1968, 1990 Matthew Jones.
All Rights Reserved. Used by Permission.

"On July 11, 1963, there was a soldier boy that came home to Danville. He saw what was going on and he had on his uniform. The Secretary of Defense issued a statement: 'You can go overseas and fight in a uniform, but you can't come back over here picketing and demonstrating in your uniform. That's un-American.'

So he got up at a mass meeting and said, 'I'm an American fighting man. I'm gonna defend my country as long as I can, and if I can defend my country overseas, why don't you set my people free?'"

Matthew Jones - SNCC

I'm a de - mon - strat - ing G. I. from Fort Bragg, the way they treat my peo - ple, Lord, it makes me mad.__ You know that I____ could-n't sit still be-cause my home_ is in Dan - ville.

CHORUS: (repeat after each verse)
I'm a demonstrating G. I. from Fort
    Bragg
And the way they treat my people, Lord,
    it makes me mad.
You know that I couldn't sit still
Because my home is in Danville.

I came home one Friday night,
I saw my sister fighting for her rights
I said, "Keep on Sis, and I'll be back
Standing tall in my boots so black."

Sitting in camp I read the paper
I said to my sargeant, "I'll see you
    later,"
I caught the bus and came on home
"I told you Sis, you wouldn't be alone."

I got arrested on Sunday ever,
The policeman said, "You've been
    overseas,
But don't you forget one simple fact,
That your skin is still black."

I was bound in jail for over a week
All I got was some beans to eat,
On a rusty tray, I was fed
And I slept on an iron bed.

Secretary of Defense, MacNamara
Said, "Come on Boy, what's the
    matter?
I don't care if you fight for freedom
But please take off your uniform."

I said, "Well I'm an American
    fighting man,
And I'll defend my country as long
    as I can,
But if I can defend it overseas,
Why can't you set my people free?"

Come on army, air force and navy,
Come on you soldiers, and don't be lazy,
If you want to integrate,
Come on down here and demonstrate.

Atlanta, Georgia, proclaims itself "a city too busy to hate." Still the Civil Rights organizations with headquarters there are working to force the city beyond tokenism.

Oginga Odinga

"Back on December 21, 1963, the State Department decided they were gonna send a Kenyan Diplomat named Oginga Odinga on an integrated tour of Atlanta, Georgia. Now we all know Atlanta, Georgia, is not integrated. So when they were planning his tour, they kinda bypassed the SNCC office, 'cause they know we're gonna show him exactly where it is ... we're gonna show him where the ghettoes are, tell him about the schools in three shifts and all this kinda thing. So since they wouldn't bring Mr. Oginga Odinga to us, we went to Mr. Oginga Odinga. We took some freedom records and some song books up to the Peachtree Manor -- that's one of the integrated hotels in Atlanta -- it ain't but about two! And we were able to bring the word of freedom to Mr. Oginga Odinga. And we sang 'We Shall Overcome'. And Mr. Odinga then said the Swahili word for freedom, Uhuru!

It's a funny thing about that word freedom. It doesn't make any difference if its Swahili, Japanese, Chinese, English or French, it's got that certain ring to it. So we just marched right out of the Peachtree Manor and over to the peacefully segregated Toddle House that was next door. And we sat in. The waitress had the nerve to tell us, 'Sorry, but we don't serve colored people here.' Now, what did she want to say that for? We just sat right down.

We sort of thank Mr. Odinga for revitalizing the movement in Atlanta. From this incident, we wrote a song which we call Oginga Odinga. "

Matthew Jones - SNCC

Verse

We went down to the Peach-tree Ma-nor to see O-gin-ga O-din-ga. The po-lice say "What's the mat-ter" to see O-gin-ga O-din-ga. The po-lice he look might-y hard at O-gin-ga O-din-ga. He got scared 'cause he was an ex-Mau-Mau, to see O-gin-ga O-din-ga.

Chorus

O-gin-ga O-din-ga, O-gin-ga O-din-ga, O-gin-ga O-din-ga of Ken-ya. *(spoken)* *(who)* O-

gin - ga O - din - ga, O - gin - ga, O - din - ga, O -

gin - ga O - din - ga of Ken - ya. Uh - hu -

hu - hu - ru. *(Haaa!)* Uh - hu - hu - hu -

ru. *(Haaa!)* Free - dom now. _____

(Haaa!) Free - dom now. _____ *(Haaa!)*

Following verses sung to first two lines of verse melody.

We went down to the Peachtree Manor to see Oginga Odinga.
The police say, 'what's the matter?' to see Oginga Odinga.
The police he look mighty hard at Oginga Odinga
He got scared 'cause he was an ex-Mau-Mau, to see Oginga Odinga.

CHORUS:
Oginga, Odinga, Oginga Odinga, Oginga Odinga, of Kenya, who?
Oginga Odinga, Oginga Odinga, Oginga Odinga of Kenya,
Uh-hu-hu-hu-ru   haaa!
Uh-hu-hu-hu-ru   haaa!
Freedom now..ow..oww,   haaa!
Freedom now..ow..oww,   haaa!

Oginga say 'look-a here, what's going on down in Selma?
If you white folks don't straighten up, I'm gonna call Jomo Kenyatta!'

CHORUS

The white folks down in Mississippi will knock you on your rump.
And if you holler Freedom, you'll wind up in the swamp!

CHORUS

The Prophecy
Of A SNCC Field Secretary

Words & music: Matthew Jones
© 1963, 1968, 1990 Matthew Jones.
All Rights Reserved. Used by Permission.

"Around the year 1990, I don't like to be a fortune-teller, but I hope we have a little freedom by then. And most of us here will be grandparents by then. Your grandchildren will ask you what you did back in the 1960s. Now we don't want you telling no lies. Don't be saying, 'I led the demonstrations in Birmingham,' when you know you didn't do a thing ... probably sitting up in New York the whole time.

So we have a song called 'The Prophecy of a SNCC Field Secretary.' This grandfather is sitting back telling his grandchildren what he did."

Matthew Jones, speaking at a SNCC conference

Verse
Am

Come here child, sit on my knee, let me

E7   Am

tell you how_ we got free, ___ It all start-ed a

long time a - go___ in nine - teen six -
ty. T'was the Stu - dent Non - vio - lent Co -
or - din - at - ing Com - mit - tee, The Stu - dent Non -
vio - lent Co - or - din - at - ing Com - mit - tee.

Hum behind narration

mm _____

SPOKEN

What happened in 1960, Grandpa? How we got free?

Come here, child, and let me tell you how we all got free,
It all happened a long time ago, in 1960.

CHORUS

It was the Student Nonviolent Coordinating Committee,
The Student Nonviolent Coordinating Committee.

> How'd it all get started, Grandpa?
> You mean to tell me after I got all these schools
> integrated, you're gonna ask me that? I should
> be asking you.
> But I don't know, grandpa.
> Well, I'll tell you then.

It all started in North Carolina, the city of Greensboro,
When some students at A & T decided to stop the white man's terror.

Grandpa, what's all this terror?
Well, let me think...

Segregation was the terror, the students fought this sin,
They used a powerful weapon they called the sit-in.

You know whose white folks really got scared.
What were they scared of, Grandpa?
They really got scared of...

The Student Nonviolent Coordinating Committee... etc.

What were some of their names, Grandpa?
Their names? You mean outside of me?
Yeah, grandpa.
Well, ah... John Lewis, they said he did all the
work, he was the Chairman. But really I was the
chairman underneath, you know how it is.
There was Charles Sherrod...

I remember a long time ago when things were mighty hard.
Up popped a nonviolent man, his name was Charles Sherrod, of

The Student Nonviolent Coordinating Committee... etc.

You know, I'm trying to think of who the Exec-
utive Secretary was... Never seem to remember
that fellow's name...

I thought you told me you were the chairman,
Grandpa?
I told you I was the chairman underneath. You
know you always have someone underneath doing all
the work. I didn't make the history books because I believe in sharing. I'm trying to think
of his name...

You mean you were the 'undercover Uncle Tom...'

You know this younger generation is going wild.
We wanted integration, we didn't want you to
be a dis-grace. Let me see if I can think of
his name...

Freedom, freedom... it's a shame, I can't remember his name,
Freedom, his name was Jim Forman, of

The Student Nonviolent Coordinating Committee... etc.

"In February, 1964, freedom workers were picketing Leb's restaurant in Atlanta. Thousands of passers-by, diners-out, and spectators crowded the four corners of the intersection. Demonstrators lined the two sides of the street. Suddenly an old man dressed in the red-piped, white satin robes of a Klan Cyclops limped through the narrow aisle of the sidewalk between restaurant and curb, leading a line of white-sheeted followers and a half dozen shirt-sleeved boys and men.

"Reporters, police, and spectators watched pop-eyed with apprehension as the white line moved valiant and stony-faced through the two dense, predominantly black walls of demonstrators. The Negro youngsters, after a loaded pause, sang 'We Shall Overcome.'

"The second or third time through, several Klansmen called out their slogans against the rising assault of music:
        'I'm a white man and proud of it!'
        'Niggers, go home!'
        'Kill the niggers!'

"'Black and white together, black and white together...' sang the laughing Negroes, most of them now dancing as they clapped. The music swelled and pounded louder, faster, and more aggressive, and the twisting girls and laughing boys danced and clapped closer and closer to the Klan.

"The young voices sang at the angry white faces, 'we shall brothers be...we shall brothers be...we shall brothers be, someday...' Another line of Klansmen crossing the street was infiltrated. Several Negro boys had borrowed white table cloths from Leb's, draped them over their dark heads, and slipped into the white line to march grinning with the Klansmen.

"The singing went on for hours, until many of us thought the poor Klansmen would, indeed, be overcome by the volume of the music, the power of the beat, and the hilarity of the ridicule."

Margaret Long, "Let Freedom Sing"
The Progressive, November 1965

"On other days, when the Klan wasn't 'integrating' the line in front of Leb's they would picket down the street at Herron's, a restaurant which served black and white. On one of those days I was running back and forth taking photos of both groups when, halfway between the two, I suddenly spotted this little girl walking along with her message written on a paper napkin.'

Ken Thompson, photographer
National Council of Churches

AMERICUS

When demonstrations began in Americus, young people were arrested by the hundreds. When the city jail was full, they were transported to stockades about a mile out of town.

"The boys went around front and kept the guard busy by talking to him. I crawled around the back and shot pictures through the bars in the rear. All the girls had been arrested in demonstrations in Americus. Some had been in the stockade a few days, others had been there for three weeks; they had no furniture, blankets or clothing other than what they had been arrested in. The toilet was clogged and gave off a smell strong enough to be sickening outside the building. The only source of water for washing or drinking was a dripping shower head. Their daily food consisted of four cold hamburgers each in the morning. When I saw them they were in good spirits."

Danny Lyon, SNCC photographer

You Should Have Been There

Adaption of spiritual by
Virginia Davis & Amanda Bowens

I said you, you, you should-a been there,

You, you, you should-a been there I said you, you, you should-a been there to ___ roll, free-dom, roll. ___ Come on and roll, roll free-dom, roll, roll free-dom, roll, roll free-dom, roll, roll free-dom, I want to get my free-dom be-fore I die, roll, free-dom roll. ___

I say you, you, you should-a been there,
You, you, you should-a been there,
I said you, you, you should have been there
To roll, freedom, roll.

LEAD	GROUP
Come on and roll	roll freedom
Roll	roll freedom
Roll	roll freedom
Roll	roll freedom

I want to get my freedom, before I die
Roll, freedom, roll.

I said, Wallace, you should have been there,
Wallace... etc.

I said, Lyndon, you should have been there,
Lyndon... etc.

I Ain't Scared A' Your Jail

Words: Lester Cobb
Music: traditional ("The Old Grey Mare")

"You know for so long the white man in the South used the jails to scare Negroes. They've lynched a lot of Negroes and there have been many, many cases where Negroes have been killed and their bodies mutilated, and nothing has been done about it. The Federal Government has refused to do anything. If you go to the court house and try to register they tell you,

'If you live on my plantation, I'm gonna get you thrown off. And I'm gonna get the sheriff to throw you in jail and throw the key away. '

But in Mississippi we had a Freedom Day. One lady brought her little son. He had a sign, say: I'M TOO YOUNG TO VOTE, BUT MY MOTHER WANT TO VOTE. A policeman called him over and said,

'If you don't pull off that sign and throw it away, boy, I'm gonna throw you in jail. '

The little boy remembered the song that we sing, and he looked up to the policeman and said,

'Mister, I ain't scared of your jail, 'cause I want my freedom! '"

Sam Block - SNCC

150

I ain't scared of your jail because I want my freedom,
I want my freedom, I want my freedom,
I ain't scared of your jail because I want my freedom,
I want my freedom now.

We'll march downtown because.... etc.

We'll go to jail because....

I served ninety days because...
　　　　　　　　　　　　　"You know in all parts of the South
they use dogs and sic 'em on people, and they use cattle prods.
Not only that, but they beat you upside the head with sticks.
They squirt water on you with a big hose. So sometimes we sing:"

I ain't scared of your dogs because...

I ain't scared of your sticks because...

I ain't scared of your hose because...
　　　　　　　　　　　　　"And sometimes they tell us, 'Well,
since you ain't scared of nothin, I'm gonna go back to the old
Southern tradition -- I'm gonna blow your brains out.' So we sing:"

I don't mind dying because....
　　　　　　　　　　　　　"And while things are going on in
Mississippi, people are doing things in other places. In Birming-
ham they sing:"
I ain't scared of no Bull* because...
We'll never turn back until....
I ain't scared of your jails because....

*Bull Conner

151

Nothing But A Soldier

Words and Music: Charles Sherrod

*"For the first time in our history a major social movement,
shaking the nation to its bones, is being led by youngsters ...
To be with them, walking a picket line in the rain in Hatties-
burg, or sleeping on a cot in a cramped 'office' in Greenville;
to watch them walk out of the stone jailhouse in Albany; to see
them jabbed by electric prod poles and flung into paddy wagons
in Selma; or to link arms and sing at the close of a church
meeting in the Delta -- is to feel the presence of greatness. It
is a greatness that comes from their relationship to history,
and it does not diminish when they are discovered to be human:
to make mistakes or feel fear, to act with envy, or hostility
or even violence.*

*All Americans owe them a debt. Theirs was the silent genera-
tion until they spoke, the complacent generation until they
marched and sang, the money-seeking generation until they re-
nounced comfort and security to fight for justice in the dank
and dangerous hamlets of the Black Belt."*

Howard Zinn, <u>SNCC: The New Abolitionists</u>

Verse

When I was a ba - by, black as I could
One day Mis - ter Char - ley, need - ed him a

be, Ma - ma held me close - ly,
maid, No more could my moth - er stay and

1. firm - ly on her knee.
2. rock me as her

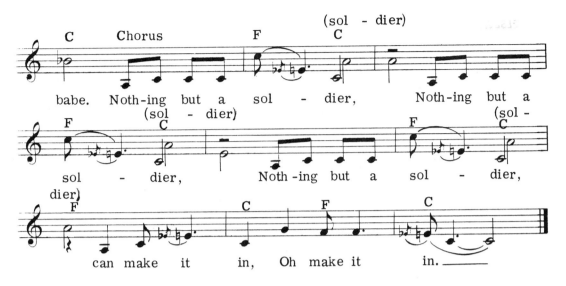

When I was a baby, black as I could be
Mama held me closely, firmly on her knee.
One day Mister Charley needed him a maid
No more could my mother stay and rock me as her babe.

CHORUS: (after each verse)
Nothing but a soldier, nothing but a soldier,
Nothing but a soldier can make it in.

Daddy never knew me, never wiped my tears,
Never saw me crying, never knew my fears
Working for the white man, sun-up 'till sun-down,
Come home wet and tired, he would always wear a frown.

I became a young man, proud as I could be
Used to hear them saying, 'Hang him on a tree,'
Tree limb couldn't hold me, segregation tried,
Jumped the gun for freedom, getting closer every stride.

Folks say don't go marching without an alibi,
But I say give me freedom before the day I die,
We don't need the H-bomb, rockets do not serve,
We have got non-violence, packs more power for every nerve.

Hoses were a-spurting, police everywhere,
Dragged me to the wagon, stripped to underwear,
Dogs tore off my clothing, cow prods burnt my flesh,
Cops beat me with blackjacks, they were stomping on my chest.

Blood ran down my forehead, blood ran down my back,
Threw me in the jailhouse, face down on the rock,
Told Judge Jim Crow slowly, I may not be brave,
You can jail my body, but I'll never be your slave.

Most of the publicity in the South is given to the big demonstrations when they reach a crisis stage. A quieter operation, which rarely receives notice, is also at work. In 1962, the Southern Christian Leadership Conference took over the Highlander Experiment in Basic Education -- the Citizenship School. Under the direction of Mrs. Septima Clark, the citizenship school idea has spread across the South.

More than 1,400 persons have received one week of intensified training in adult literacy methods and basic understanding of politics, and have returned to eleven southern states to share their newly acquired knowledge with their neighbors.

According to SCLC, ''the curriculum has changed from the basic reading and writing program to one including: Simple Banking, Consumer Economics, The Importance of the Precinct Meeting, Implementation of the Civil Rights Bill, Negro History, Planned Parenthood, and Federally Assisted Programs. The change is in keeping with new problems as they appear in the various areas of the South.

In 1964 the work paid off in big numbers. The November 3rd election saw Negroes from remote rural areas standing in line early in the morning waiting to cast a ballot for the first time in their lives. This happened all across the South. It showed the courage that had been instilled in these people who earlier feared jailings, beatings, and other reprisals. They also knew why they needed to vote.''

SCLC newsletter

Go Ahead

Traditional spiritual adapted by
citizenship school ladies from South Carolina

Go a - head, and go a - head, There is

some - thing tell - ing me to go a - head.

LEAD	GROUP
Go ahead	go ahead
Go ahead	go ahead
Something's telling me go ahead	
Go ahead	go ahead
Go ahead	go ahead
There's something telling me go ahead.	
Pray a prayer	Pray a prayer
And go ahead	go ahead
Something's telling me... etc.	
Sing a song	sing a song
And go ahead... etc.	
Cast your vote	cast your vote
And go ahead... etc.	

Up Over My Head

Adaption of gospel song by Betty Mae Fikes

This is an upbeat gospel version of the old spiritual "Over My Head." Betty Mae Fikes of Selma, Alabama, adapted it and introduced it at a Sing for Freedom Conference in Atlanta in 1964 -- a gathering of freedom singers and song-leaders from across the South.

lieve there's a God___ some - where.___

LEAD

Up above my head
I see freedom in the air
Up above my head
I see freedom in the air
Up above my head
I see freedom in the air
And I really do believe, I said I really do believe,
There's a God somewhere.

GROUP

Up above my head
I see freedom in the air
Up above my head
I see freedom in the air
Up above my head
I see freedom in the air

Up above my head, I hear praying in the air... etc.

Up above my head, I hear singing in the air...

Up above my head, I hear music in the air...

If my mother won't go, I'm gonna go anyhow...

If you can't go, let your children go...

If my brother can't go, don't let him hinder me...

Up above my head, I see freedom in the air...

FREEDOM IS
A CONSTANT STRUGGLE

The Mississippi Project

Why Was The Darkie Born?

Traditional - Adaptions
by James Bevel & Bernice Reagon

James Bevel heard an old man sing this song in Mississippi.
He asked where it came from, but the old man didn't know.

Mom - my,__ why was the dark - ie __ born?

Mom - my,__ why was the dark - ie __ born?

Some - bod - y had to pick__ the__ cot - ton,

some-bod - y had to pull__ the__ corn, Some-bod - y had to

build a great__ na - tion, and that's why the dark - ie was a-

born, that's why the dark - ie was__ born.

Mommy, why was the Darkie born?
Mommy, why was the Darkie born?
Somebody had to pick the cotton,
Somebody had to pull the corn,
Somebody had to build a great nation,
That's why the Darkie was born.
That's why the Darkie was born.

Mommy, why was the Darkie born? (2x)
Somebody had to cry at midnight,
Somebody had to weep and moan,
Somebody had to love everybody,
That's why the Darkie was born (2x)

162

Mommy...
Somebody had to beat the drums
Somebody had to blow the horn
Somebody had to sing the blues
That's....

Mommy....
Somebody had to go to jail,
Somebody had to walk a picket line,
Somebody had to fight for freedom,
That's...

"My feeling about the song in that the Darkie was created by white people. A group of people were brought over from Africa and everything that made them what they were was stripped from them. They made a Negro -- a colored man -- a Darkie. The question is why? Why was it necessary to have a Darkie? Why couldn't we have retained the word African, as the Italian people are still Italians and the Spanish people are still Spanish? Why was it necessary for the white man to make a new person -- a Darkie?"

Bernice Reagon - SNCC

Mom-my,___ why were the dark - ies born?

Mom-my,___ why were the dark - ies born?

Some-bod-y had to plant___ the cot-ton ____

Some-bod-y had to pull the corn, Some-bod-y had to

work___ for noth-in'___ That's why the dark-ies were___ born.

Verse-Very free

(4) Oh, Lord,___ I_____ am try - in'

work-in' hard_ un - til the day, When_my

ba - by won't have ____ to wor - ry_____ 'bout

be - in' born black this way._____

Mommy...
Somebody had to cry at midnight
Somebody had to weep and moan
Somebody had to sing the blues, child,
That's....

Oh Lord, I'm trying
Working hard until the day
When my baby won't have to worry
'Bout being born black this way.

Mommy....
Somebody had to plant the cotton,
Somebody had to pull the corn,
Somebody had to build this nation,
That's why.....

Mommy, why were the Darkies born?
Mommy, why were the Darkies born?
Somebody had to plant the cotton,
Somebody had to pull the corn,
Somebody had to work for nothin',
That's why the Darkies were born.

Come here my little baby,
Sit on your mama's knee
And I will try to tell you
Why your Ma ain't free.

Freedom Train A' Comin'

Adaption of union song

Hear__ that - a free - dom train a -
com - ing, com - ing, com - ing, Hear that free - dom train a -
com - ing, com - ing, com - ing, Hear that free - dom train a -
com-ing, com-ing, com-ing, Get on board, oh,__ oh get on board.

Hear that Freedom Train a' comin', comin', comin'
Hear that Freedom Train a' comin', comin', comin'
Hear that Freedom Train a' comin', comin', comin'
Get on board, get on board.

It'll be carryin' nothing but freedom, freedom, freedom (3x)
Get on board, get on board.

They'll be comin' by the thousand, thousand, thousand (3x)
Get on board, get on board.

It'll be carryin' freedom fighters, fighters, fighters, (3x)
Get on board, get on board.

It'll be carryin' registered voters, voters, voters (3x)
Get on board, get on board.

It'll be rollin' through Mississippi, Mississippi (3x)
Get on board, get on board.

Hear that Freedom Train a' comin'....

"It's no use of you being worried, trying to turn back. It's no use of you saying 'I'm not in this mess!' because if you were born with your skin black, you were automatically born in the mess. So you just might as well come on and get on the Freedom Train. Get on board, children, get on board."

Sam Block, SNCC

THE SUMMER PROJECT

"The 1964 Mississippi Summer Project was an operation like nothing in the nation's history. Seven hundred college students from all over the country showed up at Oxford, Ohio, for an orientation session organized by the National Council of Churches. There, young veterans of the Black Belt tried to give them realistic pictures of the dangers they faced. They were taught how to protect themselves from injury without responding violently. They talked passionately about their own fears, their indecision, their dreams. Then they climbed into buses and cars and headed South.

"The volunteers were mostly white, northern, middle-class. The staff people -- mainly SNCC, some CORE, a few SCLC --were generally Negro, Southern, sent by lower-class parents to Negro colleges, from which they darted off into the movement. Together, in clusters, they fanned out across Mississippi.

"Besides the students there were several hundred Northern professional people-- doctors, nurses, lawyers, ministers, teachers. The doctors and nurses were part of a new phenomenon which seemed to grow up overnight, called the Medical Committee for Human Rights. The lawyers formed an efficient corps such as had never been seen before in the civil rights troubles of this decade. As for the ministers, they were everywhere: on picket lines, in Freedom Houses, at mass meetings.

"The Mississippi Summer had an effect impossible to calculate..."

Howard Zinn, SNCC, The New Abolitionists

"The most devastating affront to the old order in Mississippi and the most momentous challenge to the prevailing caste system, has been the fact of nearly a thousand white summer visitors living and working amiably with Negro families."

James Silver, Foreword to Letters from Mississippi

"Man like I don't even believe what I just did. You really had to be here to appreciate it. I took a bath. But no ordinary bath 'cause there's no running water. No, we take this bucket out in the back yard and fill it with water warmed over a fire. It's pitch black so we shine Mr. Clark's truck lights on the bucket. Then I strip down naked and stand in the bucket wash. That is the way you take a bath around here."

Letters from Mississippi

169

"Everyday this week the men of the community hammered and poured cement. At noon, about seven or eight women all gathered at the center with fried chicken, fish, salad, gallons of cool-aid and apple turnovers, and served them to the men, we teachers, and each other. It is a thing of beauty to see us all work together. Tuesday and Wednesday was the laying of the sub-floor. Two men cut the wood, two or three teenage boys and girls laid the wood down and hammered it in, a few more are bringing more wood. It should be up by Saturday.

"The land was given by a local man for 'the sum of one dollar', and deeds were drawn up. The teenagers are selling refreshments to raise money for the center, as well as membership cards for a dollar. It will hold the library, a snack-bar office space and recreation area...

"The men (and some of us when we have time) work on the building up to ten hours a day with a 100 degree sun beating down and the humidity so high one's clothing becomes soaking wet after only a few minutes work. The building is guarded at night because these people, after having had their homes shot into and having a couple of crosses burned in the middle of their community during the last few months, do not intend to have all their hard work go up in flames right away..."

Letters from Mississippi

"The major contribution of the Mississippi Summer Project were the 'freedom schools'.

"The object of the Freedom School was not to cram a prescribed amount of factual material into young minds, but to give them that first look into new worlds which would, some day if not immediately, lead them to books and people and ideas not found in the everyday lives of Mississippi Negroes."

Howard Zinn, SNCC, The New Abolishionists

Another major portion of the summer went to canvassing and registering voters for the Mississippi Freedom Democratic Party.

"Yesterday we canvassed...One lady couldn't work because she had cut her leg badly with the hoe while chopping cotton, and her leg was full of stitches. She lived in a two-room unpainted shack (kindly provided by the management). You climbed on the porch by stepping on a bucket -- there were huge holes in the porch for the unwary. The woman was sitting dejectedly on the bed as she couldn't walk very well. She was surrounded by shy children, some of them naked. We tried to explain what Freedom Registration meant -- it seemed like a rather abstract approach to her problems..."

Letters from Mississippi

"Dear Mom,

"I have become so close to the family I am staying with -- eleven people -- that Mrs. H. finally paid me a great compliment. She was introducing me to one of her Negro women friends and said, 'This is Nancy, my adopted daughter!'

"All evening I have little children crawling over me and big boys, 16, my buddies, combing my hair, confiding in me, appreciating me, because I will open my heart and mind to them and listen and care for them and show my concern. I may be sex- and love-starved, as some like to picture me, but at least I have faced the problem and have found my own inner peace by being with people who have not forgotten how to love.

"Really, to tell the honest truth, I am just a little bit tired of hearing you and others, and for a long time even myself, think, worry, discuss, write and talk about all the deep down psychological reasons for your personal problems. When I see these simple people living lives of relative inner peace, love, honor, courage, and humor, I lose patience with people who sit and ponder their belly buttons..."

Letters from Mississippi

"The Mississippi Caravan of Music was a cultural arm of the Summer Project. Singing is the backbone and balm of this movement. Somehow you can go on in the face of violence and death, cynicism and inaction of the FBI, the indifference of the Federal Government when you can sing with your band of brothers.

"Those Caravan singers who could stay for a period longer than a week, spent two or more days at each project. Others went from place to place on a rather hectic schedule. A typical Caravan day would begin with the singers participating in a class on Negro history at the Freedom School. They showed that freedom songs were sung back in the days of slavery -- how some songs even blueprinted the way to freedom on the underground railroad. The singers demonstrated the important contribution of Negro music in every aspect of American musical and cultural history. For children who have been brainwashed by the public school system to accept the myth of their own inferiority, this was an exhilarating revelation. For the majority of adults as well as children it was the first time they had heard of such great musical artists as Leadbelly and Big Bill Broonzy. For many, the music they had learned to be ashamed of was given new stature by the visiting musicians.

"Completing a program at one Freedom School the Caravan group would travel on to another. There they would hold a workshop informally with the students in the afternoon. After time out for dinner there would be a mass rally or a hootenanny that might last three hours. It seemed to me that the farther out in the country and the more ramshackle the wooden church, the greater was the singing.

"Always the singers would return to Freedom House late at night and sing on into the early hours of the morning with the civil rights workers who had little other opportunity to just relax and let off steam.

"Sometimes Caravan Activities stimulated local white people to participate for the first time in an integrated function (non-violently that is!). A number of white Mississippians turned out for concerts that Julius Lester, Len Chandler and Cordell Reagon gave on the Gulf Coast. When Pete Seeger sang in McComb, two white college students came to hear him. Several days later they had dinner with some of the civil rights workers. Soon afterward, when Pete sang in Jackson, four students from Ole Miss attended. They, too, were so impressed that they showed up a few days later in the Jackson COFO office, expressing interest in the Freedom Schools. All of this took considerable courage on the part of these local white youths."

Bob Cohen, director
Mississippi Caravan of Music

Father's Grave

Words & music: Len H. Chandler Jr.
© 1964 by Fall River Music Inc.
All Rights Reserved. Used by Permission.

Len and Cordell Reagon travelled together during the summer Caravan through Mississippi and other areas of the South. They visited the house where Cordell grew up in Waverly, Tennessee. Cordell had talked often about not getting to his father's funeral on time. They went to the graveyard and cut the weeds down over the grave. They talked about freedom and about whether their children would have to go through the difficult changes they were going through in the next generation.

This is a personal song, yet its chorus speaks for many in the movement.

1. With my swing blade in my hand As I looked a-cross the land And_ thought of all the pla-ces that I'd been,___ Of that old house that I called home Where I'd

al - ways been a - lone And of that weed - y___ grave that___
held___ my clos - est kin.___ And as I
cut the weeds from o'er my fa - ther's grave, fa-ther's grave, I ___
swore no child I bore would be ___ a slave.

With my swing blade in my hand, as I looked across the land
And thought of all the places that I'd been,
Of that old house that I called home,
Where I'd always been alone
And of that weedy grave that held my closest kin.

CHORUS: (after each verse)
And as I cut the weeds from o'er my father's grave, father's grave,
I swore no child I bore would be a slave.

Oh, the old house was a shell, there were weeds around the well,
And I touched the rusty hinge that held no door
And the roof was caving in, It was always sort of thin,
And I found the place where the ash pan burned the floor.

I thought of all the glad and the good times that I had
With my pockets full of purple plums each fall
When the yard was wide and clean and the grass was short & green
Now the underbrush has laid its claim to all.

It made me feel so bad, lost the best friend that I had
And I didn't get to hear the preacher pray
Yes, and I was only eight, no, I can't recall the date
Nor the reason I was late, but a funeral just can't wait
And when I got to church they were rolling him away.

In Rosedale, Mississippi
there is one white doctor

And this doctor doesn't come
whenever peoples call

This doctor comes
later on.

But in Rosedale see
there isn't any place
For the
peoples

to assemble
and talk about
the way peoples feel.

AND WHAT THEY CAN DO
About the doctor
And the school
And being Very Hungry
ALL DAY.

Because there isn't any money
Two dollars maybe
For a whole day's work
in the fields.

That's ALL.

And if you get sick
The doctor won't come

And if you get well
You got to go back out
To the fields

But you don't have to
Pretty soon.

Pretty soon
A whole lot of peoples
Won't go.

A Whole Lot of Peoples
is Strong.

A Whole Lot Of Peoples Is Strong

Mrs. Ida Mae Lawrence Rosedale, Mississippi

"The ones that are going into this is the young, hot niggers, not our good old Mississippi niggers. These freedom workers are low-down snakes in the weeds."

O. C. Allen, farmer in Leake County

I Want My Freedom

Tune: You are My Sunshine
Words: The Rev. Mrs. Elvira Bailey

CHORUS:
I want my freedom, I want my
      freedom,
I want to be a free, free man,
I want my freedom, I want my
      freedom
I want to be a free, free man.

The other day dear, as I was
      walking,
I read a sign 'no colored allowed'
I read that sign dear, I read it over,
And I hung my head and cried.

In this America, new things are
      happening
To make the white man finally see
That we are human, that we are equal
And that we shall, we shall be free.

In this America, new things are
      happening
To make the black man finally see
That they must fight dear, that they
      must fight dear,
If they are ever to be free.

It Isn't Nice

Words: Malvina Reynolds
Music: Malvina Reynolds & Barbara Dane
© 1964 Schroder Music (ASCAP),
Berkeley CA 94704. Used by Permission.

This song was introduced in Mississippi by Barbara Dane and Judy Collins on their trips with the Caravan of Music. It is still widely sung there.

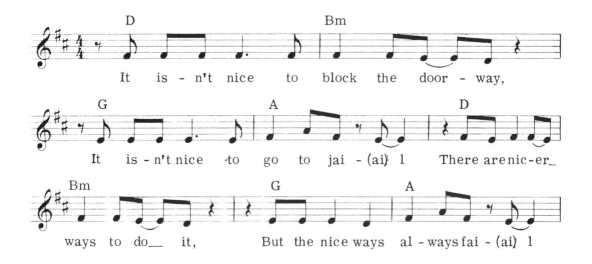

It is-n't nice to block the door - way,
It is-n't nice to go to jai - (ai) l There are nic-er
ways to do__ it, But the nice ways al - ways fai - (ai) l

Chorus

It is-n't nice, it is-n't nice,_ You told us once,_ You told us twice,_ But if that's free-dom's price_ we don't mind._

No, no, no, no_ no_

Final chorus ending

We don't mind _ We don't mind _

etc. (ad lib.)

It isn't nice to block the doorway,
It isn't nice to go to jail,
There are nicer ways to do it
But the nice ways always fail
It isn't nice, it isn't nice
You told us once, you told us twice
But if that's freedom's price,
We don't min d.......no, no, no, no,
   no,
We don't mind.

It isn't nice to dump the groceries,
Or to sleep in on the floor,
Or to shout or cry of freedom
In the hotel or the store,
It isn't nice, it isn't nice,
You told us once, you told us twice,
But if that's freedom's price,
We don't mind...

Well, we've tried negotiations
And the token picket line,
Mister Charley didn't see us
And he might as well be blind;
When you deal with men of ice,
You can't deal with ways so nice,
But if that's freedom's price,
We don't mind...

They kidnapped boys in Mississippi,
They shot Medgar in the back,
Did you say that wasn't proper?
Did you stand out on the track?
You were quiet just like mice,
Now you say that we're not nice,
Well, if that's freedom's price,
We don't mind...

It isn't nice to block the doorway,
It isn't nice to go to jail,
There are nicer ways to do it
But the nice ways always fail
It isn't nice, it isn't nice
You told us once you told us twice,
Thanks buddy, for your advice,
Well it that's freedom's price,
We don't mind.....
WE DON'T MIND

"Never go any places where there aren't at least two roads so that people who follow you in have to watch two exits when you leave."

SNCC worker

"In this summer the stranger is the enemy, and the men of Mississippi wait and watch for him. In khaki pants and straw hat they stand their watch against the civil rights workers across the Delta counties.

"By night they ride dipping roads in the hill country to the east where that fatal plant, the kudzu vine, grows everywhere strangling grass and tree. Along Route 19 they drive through Neshoba County's scrub oak and scraggly pine forests without headlights when the moon is bright and the mist is sparse and patchy.

"For the Negroes, fear makes the night wakeful. Negro farmers check their guns and count their children as the night comes on. The short nights of summer are long -- longer than ever now because the white civil rights workers are living hidden among the Negro farm folk."

Nicholas Von Hoffman
Mississippi Notebook

"We are now in the midst of the 'long, hot summer' of agitation which was promised to the Innocent People of Mississippi by the savage blacks and their community masters...

"There is no racial problem here in this state. Our system of strict segregation permits the two races to live in close proximity and harmony with each other and eliminates any racial problem...

"Bi-racial groups are the greatest danger we face in this State today. We are not going to recognize the authority of any bi-racial group, NOR THE AUTHORITY OF ANY PUBLIC OFFICIAL WHO ENTERS INTO ANY AGREEMENT WITH ANY SUCH SOVIET ORGANIZATION.

"We Knights are working day and night to preserve Law and Order here in Mississippi, in the only way that it can be preserved; by strict segregation of the races, and the control of the social structure in the hands of the Christian, Anglo-Saxon White men, the only race on earth that can build and maintain just and stable governments. We are deadly serious about this business.

"Take heed, atheists and mongrels, we will not travel your path to Leninist Hall, but we will buy YOU a ticket to the Eternal if you insist. Take your choice, SEGREGATION, TRANQUILITY AND JUSTICE, OR BI-RACISM, CHAOS AND DEATH..."

The Klan Ledger
White Knights of the Ku Klux Klan
July, 1964

"The Student Nonviolent Coordinating Committee places a large order when it asks people to meet violence with non-violence. So far, here in Greenwood, they have been able to make their point -- that non-violence is tactically necessary in demonstrations. But SNCC has also, I think, encouraged self-protection, and it has proven difficult to discern where self-defense and 'defense of the community' are distinct from each other. To these young people, as to most, violence is not at all a last and regrettable, resort. To be violent has usually been, in the minds of Southerners, to be courageous. The boycott, powerful economic blow or not, does not satisfy the repressed urge of these young people to strike back.

"It is frightening to know that anything the opposition does they justify on bases of principle, and to realize that much of what they do is inspired by moral fervor. Playing on their sense of guilt is a dubious, even negligible weapon, it would seem. I saw this perverted moralism translated into violent action the other day when I was chased out of the white neighborhood with stones and curses, a car finally ran, me off the road and forced me to dive into a Negro's chickencoop for safety. That little gimp-legged man with the wild blue eyes who was not a good enough shot to hit me with the rocks, who ran after me down the street with his cronies, who roared after me in his car and came up onto the dirt after me with it, who swung at me with his left hand as he went by but missed again, believed that he was striking blows for freedom, among other things -- for all that is good and right. I suppose all you can do for a man like that is pray for him. Is he wicked? If he isn't, then maybe no one is and maybe that's the proper conclusion: there are no evil men in the world, only scared ones and indignant ones and hateful ones. But if there are no evil men, there is evil; you feel it come into yourself when you view these men..."

Letters from Mississippi

Mississippi Goddam

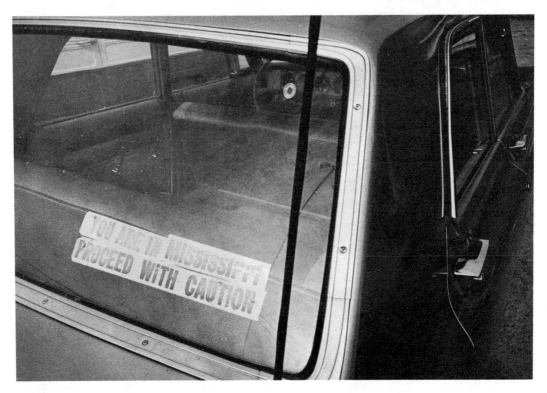

*"The Summer Project headquarters in Jackson had mimeo-
graphed a list of 'incidents' from shootings to church burnings
and traffic violation arrests, during the period of June 16 to
August 14. It covers thirty-four pages, most of them legal
size and single-spaced."*

Elizabeth Sutherland, The Nation, Sept. 14, 1964

Al - a - bam - a's got me so up-set__
Ten - nes - see made me lose my rest and Ev - 'ry-bod - y knows
a - bout Mis - sis-sip-pi god - dam. Can't you
see it, Can't you feel it, It's all in the air,____
I can't stand the pres - sure much longer some-one__ say a prayer.
Al - a - bam - a's got me so up-set,__ Ten-nes - see made me
lose my rest__ and Ev - 'ry-bod - y knows a-bout Mis - sis-sip-pi
god - dam.__ Hound dogs__
on my trail, School chil - dren sit - ting in jail,

Too slow, You're just plain rot - ten   Too slow, You're

too dam la - zy   Too slow,   Your think-ing's cra - zy

Too slow.   Where am I go - ing,   What am I do - ing,

I don't know,__   I don't know,__   Just try__ to do your

ver - y best__ Stand up, be count-ed with all the rest__ Cause

ev - 'ry-bod - y knows   a - bout Mis - sis-sip - pi god - dam.__

(For v.2, D.S. to ⊕ to Coda)

Coda

Ev - 'ry-bod - y knows   a-bout Mis-sis-sip-pi, Ev - 'ry-bod - y knows

a - bout   Al - a - ba - ma,   Ev - 'ry - bod - y knows

a - bout Mis - sis-sip - pi   god - DAM._____

Alabama's got me so upset, Tennessee made me lose my rest,
And everybody knows about Mississippi goddam.
Can't you see it, can't you feel it, it's all in the air;
I can't stand the pressure much longer, someone say a prayer.
Alabama's got me so upset, Tennessee made me lose my rest,
And everybody knows about Mississippi goddam.

Hound dogs on my trail, school children sitting in jail,
Black cat cross my path, I think every day's gonna be my last.
Lord have mercy on this land of mine, we all gonna get it in due time.
Don't belong here, I don't belong there, I even stopped believing in prayer.

Don't tell me, I'll tell you, Me and my people just about due.
I've been there, so I know, they keep on saying 'Go slow. '
That's just the trouble - too slow,
Washing the windows - too slow,
Picking the cotton - too slow,
You're just plain rotten - too slow,
You're too damn lazy - too slow,
You thinkin's crazy - too slow,
Where am I going, what am I doing, I don't know. I don't know.
Just try to do your very best,
Stand up, be counted with all the rest,
'Cause everybody knows about Mississippi goddam.

Picket lines, school boycott, try to say it's a Communist plot.
All I want is equality, for my sister and brother, my people and me.
You lied to me all these years, you told me to wash & clean my ears.
Talk real fine, just dress like a lady, and you'd stop calling me Sister Sadie.
But this whole country is corrupted with lies,
You all should die and die like flies
I don't trust you any more, you keep on saying, 'Go slow. '
That's just the trouble - too slow
Desegregation - too slow
Mass participation - too slow
Unification - too slow
Do things gradually - too slow
Will bring more tragedy - too slow

Why don't you see it, why can't you feel it?
I don't know, I don't know.
You don't have to live next to me
Just give me Equality.

Everybody knows about Mississippi,
Everybody knows about Alabama,
Everybody knows about Mississippi goddam.

"Dear folks,

"Last night I was a long time before sleeping, although I was extremely tired. Every shadow, every noise -- the bark of a dog, the sound of a car -- in my fear and exhaustion was turned into a terrorist's approach. And I believed that I heard the back door open and a Klansman walk in, until he was close by the bed. Almost paralyzed by the fear, silent, I finally shone my flashlight on the spot where I thought he was standing...I tried consciously to overcome this fear. To relax, I began to breathe deep, think the words of a song, pull the sheet up close to my neck...still the tension.

"Anyone who comes down here and is not afraid I think must be crazy as well as dangerous to this project where security is quite important. But the type of fear that they mean when they, when we, sing 'we are not afraid' is the type that immobilizes...The songs help to dissipate the fear. Some of the words in the songs do not hold real meaning on their own, others become rather monotonous -- but when they are sung in unison, or sung silently by oneself, they take on new meaning beyond words or rhythm...There is almost a religious quality about some of these songs, having little to do with the usual concept of a god. It has to do with the miracle that youth has organized to fight hatred and ignorance. It has to do with the holiness of the dignity of man. The god that makes such miracles is the god I do believe in when we sing 'God is on our side.' I know I am on that god's side, and I do hope he is on ours."

Letters from Mississippi

Freedom Is A Constant Struggle

Words & music: Roberta Slavit
© 1964 by Stormking Music Inc.
All Rights Reserved. Used by Permission.

They say that freedom is a constant struggle,
They say that freedom is a constant struggle,
They say that freedom is a constant struggle,
Oh Lord, we've struggled so long,
We must be free, we must be free.

They say that freedom is a constant crying...
Oh Lord, we've cried so long....

They say that freedom is a constant sorrow....
Oh Lord, we've sorrowed so long....

They say that freedom is a constant moaning....
Oh Lord, we've moaned so long....

They say that freedom is a constant dying....
Oh Lord, we've died so long,
We must be free, we must be free.

*"During gentle mid-June days in 1964, three lives converged
in the campus town of Oxford, Ohio, and ended on Rock Cut
Road in Neshoba County, Mississippi. Andrew Goodman, a
twenty year old Queens College student; James Chaney, a
Negro born and raised in Meridian, Mississippi; and Michael
Schwerner, a New York City social worker. On June 20th the
trio arrived in Meridian, but within twenty-four hours they had
disappeared. For six tense weeks the search for the three
missing civil rights workers went on; On August 4th their
bodies were dug out of an earthen dam.*

*Mickey Schwerner's wife and parents tried hard to have
Mickey's body buried in Mississippi along side that of James
Chaney, only to discover that interracial burials are pro-
hibited in Mississippi, unless perhaps beneath a dam.*

*When a memorial service for the three was held next to the
charred ruins of the Mt. Zion Methodist Church, Sheriff
Rainey and Deputy Price came to watch and listen. Young Ben
Chaney gave one of the talks, saying with tears running down
his cheeks, 'I want us all to stand up here together and say
just one thing. I want the Sheriff to hear this good. We ain't
scared no more of Sheriff Rainey!'"*

Jack Mendelsohn, <u>*The Martyrs*</u>

There is a street in Itta Bena called Freedom,
There is a town in Mississippi called Liberty,
There is a department in Washington called Justice.

A sign in the COFO office

"We suppose that the people who murdered Mickey and Andrew and James were not like us, not like most people in the country. I think that's a deep mistake, that we don't understand the implication of that. People keep asking me, 'Do you think that they will get convicted?' It seems that our experience will tell us that they cannot be convicted. For them to be convicted would be for society to condemn itself and that's very hard for society to do -- any society.

"The jury that votes together to decide whether or not the eighteen or twenty people who evidently got together and sat down and then planned and then got up and then murdered, that jury is like them. That's a hard thing to understand in this country."

Bob Moses speaking at the 5th Anniversary of SNCC

We Got A Thing Going On

Words and Music: SCLC

This song was made up by young people in Green County, Alabama, but it tells about the kind of "thing" going on all over the South.

"Deep in the America nobody wants to see, SNCC staffers have learned a great deal about themselves and about others. Their program is a reflection of experiences paid for by blood and pain since the sit-in movement. SNCC concentrated in the beginning on lunch counter desegregation. 'But we soon discovered', Prathia Hall says, 'that that was not where it was at.' Then we went into the Black Belt with voter registration. The people there couldn't eat at lunch counters because they were only making twenty-three cents an hour. That was where it was at.' SNCC shifted its emphasis from hamburgers to political power, using voter registration as a tool to reorganize communities and re-structure them around new axes. In out-of-the-way places, without trumpets, the original sixteen SNCC workers clawed toeholds and hung on. They went from one filthy jail to another, from one shack to another -- and as they moved, singing, their numbers grew.

Mississippi, which is criss-crossed today with a beehive of indigenous political and economic movements, is a tangible testimonial to SNCC's community organization concept."

Lerone Bennett Jr.
SNCC: Rebels With a Cause

LEAD	GROUP
We got a thing going on	
We got a thing	we got a thing going on,
We got a thing	we got a thing going on,
We got a thing going on.	

LEAD	GROUP
What kind of thing?	a voter-registration thing going on,
What kind of thing?	a voter-registration thing going on,
What kind of thing?	a voter-registration thing going on,
We got a thing going on.	

LEAD	GROUP
Tell the world	tell the world we got a thing going on...
etc.	

LEAD	GROUP
What will we get	we're gonna get our freedom...
etc.	

It has landed — it has landed in Georgia...
(Alabama)
(Mississippi)
etc.

We got a thing — we got a thing going on...

"I question America"
Mrs. Fannie Lou Hamer
1964 Democratic Convention

"The 15th Amendment of the United States Constitution commands that no person shall be deprived of the right to vote by reason of race or color. It was added to the Constitution nearly a hundred years ago. In 1867, more than 60,000 Negroes were on Mississippi's voting rolls.

"By 1892, there were only 8,500 Negroes registered. What happened between 1867 and 1892 is a nightmare in the American Dream.

"For more than a generation, in reprisal to Reconstruction, Mississippi turned life for the Negro into hell. It was a period of lynchings, armed attacks, economic harassment and other crimes -- efficiently calculated to keep the Negro away from the ballot box. The theory worked perfectly. With the opposition crushed, white Mississippians drafted a new constitution which was never submitted to the voters for ratification. The new instrument simply disenfranchised the Negro by establishing literacy qualifications which few were able to pass and poll taxes which the majority couldn't afford to pay. Since 1890, these various devices and a number of other refinements have kept more than ninety percent of Negro Mississippians in what amounts to a condition of servitude.

"In 1961, the decision was made by young freedom workers to attack the tradition that the Negro could be kept emasculated as long as he was kept politically silent. So, voter registration for Mississippi's black, second-class citizens began, first in the southwest part of the state, then in the northern Delta country. The advance has been painful and slow.

"1963 produced a mock election in Mississippi which set the tone for the 1964 Summer Project. While white Mississippians voted for a white governor, black Mississippians voted for their own man -- Aaron Henry. More than 83,000 Negroes throughout the state voted, all but a few for the first time in their lives. That proved that Negroes wanted to vote.

"The Freedom Democratic Party was established in Jackson, the state capitol, on April 26, 1964. The party was open to all races. A 'Freedom' voter-registration application was drawn up, a much-simplified version of the booby-trapped regular form. Party apparatus was organized at precinct meetings in twenty-six counties in July; thirty-five county conventions followed, and finally there was a state convention in Jackson."

From Reports - the Challenge
National Council of Churches
Commission on Religion & Race

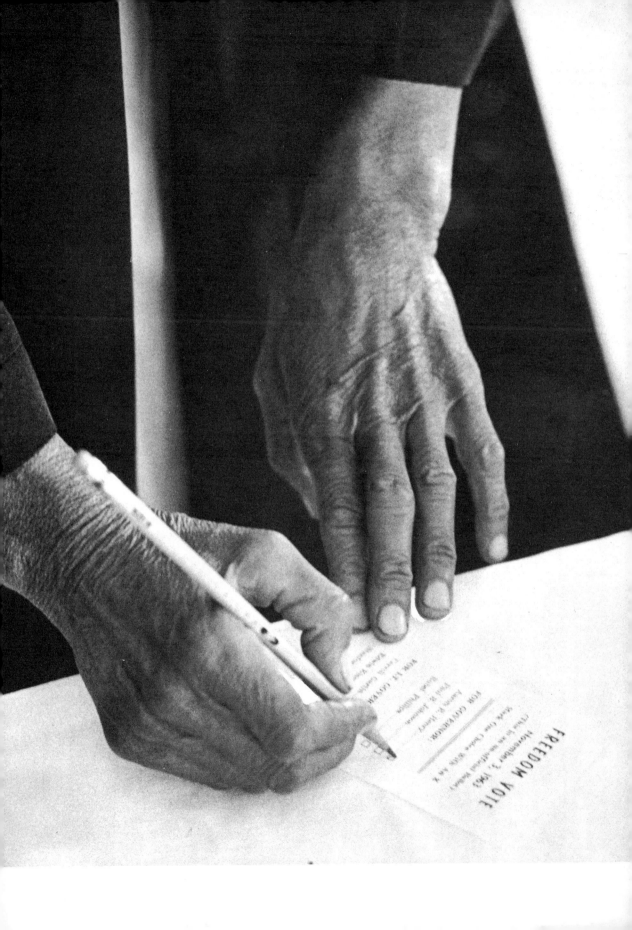

FREEDOM VOTE
November 3, 1963

(This is an unofficial ballot.)

Mark One (Index with an

FOR GOVERNOR:
Aaron E. Henry
Paul B. Johnson
Rubel Phillips

FOR LIEUTENANT
Fannie Lou Hamer

Go Tell It On The Mountain

Adaptions of old spiritual
by Mrs. Hamer & Carlton Reese

"From the floor of the State Convention of the Mississippi Democratic Party:

This is the most exciting, moving and impressive thing that I have ever had the pleasure of witnessing -- let alone be a part of.

Miss Ella Baker presented a very stirring keynote address. She put great stress upon the fact that these people here today have braved extreme danger and now must redouble their efforts to get all their neighbors to join them in this struggle for Freedom.

Right after Miss Baker's speech, there was a march of all the delegates around the convention hall -- singing freedom songs, waving American flags, banners and county signs. This was probably the most soul-felt march ever to occur in a political convention, I felt, as we marched with a mixture of sadness and joy -- of humility and pride -- of fear and courage, singing 'Go Tell it on the Mountain', 'Ain't Gonna Let Nobody Turn Me 'Round', and 'This Little Light of Mine'. You would just about have to be here to really feel and see what this means to the people who are here."

<u>*Letters from Mississippi*</u>

CHORUS:
Go tell it on the mountain, over the hills and everywhere,
Go tell it on the mountain, to let my people go.

Who's that yonder dressed in red?
Let my people go,
It must be the children Bob Moses led,
Let my people go.

Who's that yonder dressed in black?...
It must be the Uncle Toms turning back...

Who's that yonder dressed in blue?
It must be the registrars coming through...

Birmingham version

CHORUS:
Go tell it on the mountain, over the hills and everywhere*
Go tell it on the mountain, that freedom is coming soon. Halleluia

You know I would not be Governor Wallace
I'll tell you the reason why,
I'd be afraid my Lord might call me
And I would not be ready to die.
Halleluia

Oh I would not be Mayor Boutwell....

Oh I would not be Barry Goldwater....

Oh I would not be the segregationists....

*In some choruses this becomes every-every-everywhere.

In late August the Mississippi Freedom Democratic Party went to the national convention of the Democratic Party in Atlantic City, New Jersey.

"What happened between August 23 and 26, went beyond the greatest expectations of all those young people who had trudged the backroads with their registration forms, worrying about quotas. It justified all the dreams of developing indigenous leadership in black Mississippi. There, by the sea, across from a huge billboard with a picture of Barry Goldwater and the inscription 'In your heart you know he's right', a band of people from nowhere brought the machinery of a powerful national party to a halt for four days. They told their stories of oppression and terror -- Mrs. Hamer, fired the day she registered, later beaten unconscious for voter registration work -- while the Credentials Committee listened and the Mississippi regulars made feeble replies.

"The Credentials Committee finally offered a compromise (after much behind-the-scenes politicing) which provided for the seating of the regulars; the recognition of Dr. Aaron Henry and Rev. Ed King as delegates at large from the FDP and all others as honored guests; a promise that the Democratic National Committee would obligate states to select delegates for 1968 in a non-discriminatory way and that it would establish a special committee to aid states in meeting this standard.

"The Freedom Democrats rejected the compromise, in the face of arguments voiced by such national figures as Bayard Rustin and Martin Luther King. There was a sit-in on the convention floor by the FDP.

"The compromise was rejected for several reasons. The two seats were considered token recognition -- and the Negro people of Mississippi had seen too much tokenism in their time. They had come there as true representatives, not as 'delegates at large.' The compromise still recognized the regulars, despite the mass of evidence to prove they had no business there. The promises for 1968 offered no genuine relief because they referred only to Negroes already registered; even if a few Negroes could attend party meetings four years later, the people were no more likely than before to have a voice in decision making. The compromise contained no precedent for eventual recognition or patronage. To the FDP, it was a one-shot affair -- their anguish, their demands, their cause, were not."

Elizabeth Sutherland, Letters from Mississippi

"When a man has risked his life to vote, you can't offer him less than what he needs and be relevant."

Prathia Hall, SNCC

Carry It On

Some summer volunteers decided to stay on in Mississippi.

"Dear Mom and Dad,

As I write this letter I am on the roof of our headquarters observing a sunset I cannot even begin to describe. The hills of red dirt, the pine woods, the mountains and shacks silhouetted against the blood-red sun and clouds, all this and the rest of it takes my breath away. Now and at all such times I find myself possessed by a deep melancholy, a heart-rending feeling for the black and white toilers of this state; both victims of a system that they neither created nor flourish under.

There have been incidents of violence and intimidation but they hardly seem worth noting at a time like this. I only know that I must carry on this struggle that other people have died in, and that some day that system will be changed..."

Letters from Mississippi

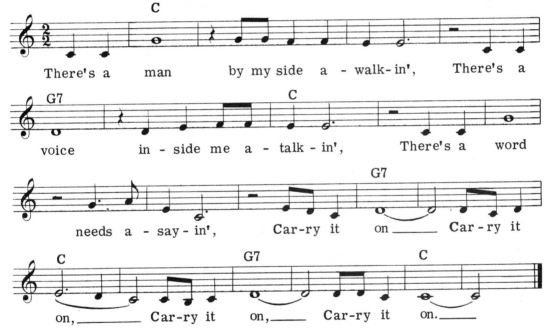

There's a man by my side a-walk-in', There's a voice in-side me a-talk-in', There's a word needs a-say-in', Car-ry it on ___ Car-ry it on, ___ Car-ry it on, ___ Car-ry it on.___

There's a man by my side walkin'
There's a voice inside me talkin',
There's a word needs a-saying',
Carry it on, carry it on,
Carry it on, carry it on.

They will tell their lyin' stories
Send their dogs to bite our bodies
They will lock us in prison,
Carry it on, carry it on,
Carry it on, carry it on.

All their lies be soon forgotten,
All their dogs will lie there rottin'
All their prison walls will crumble,
Carry it on, carry it on,
Carry it on, carry it on.

If you can't go on any longer
Take the hand held by your brother
Every victory gonna bring another,
Carry it on, carry it on,
Carry it on, carry it on.

I BEEN IN
THE STORM SO LONG

The Roots

Dance and Play Songs

Work Songs

Blues

Spirituals

The people are our teachers. People who have struggled to support themselves and large families, people who have survived in Georgia and Alabama and Mississippi, have learned some things we need to know. There is a fantastic poetry in the lives of the people who have survived with strength and nobility. I am convinced of how desparately America needs the blood transfusion that comes from the Delta of Mississippi."

Prathia Hall, SNCC

"We all know that you can't trust a Negro on a negotiating committee who doesn't like his people's music. We found that out in Birmingham."

Rev. Andrew Young, SCLC

"One of the interesting developments in the South today is a new movement for the revival of true Negro folk music and other old cultural forms, such as dance and story. The moving force comes from young Southern Negroes who have come out of the freedom movement. Possessed of an inner freedom and sense of dignity won in struggle, they no longer feel ashamed of traditions of the past and have suddenly discovered a beauty and strength in the culture of their forefathers. They have determined that it not be lost.

"The emphasis is not at all on selling the rest of the country on the value of Southern Negro culture. That has already been done.

"Negroes have given the world a universal language in their music. Everywhere people want to hear ragtime, jazz, blues, gospel music, but the root forms from which this music springs are being lost. Many Negro singers from the South draw big audiences all over the country -- some of them promoted by commercial interests seeking profits, some by sincere folklorists and folk music lovers. But the people back home still think this music is something to be ashamed of.

"The most immediate aim of this new movement is to bring the music produced by the Southern Negro back to the children of those who produced it."

Anne Braden, The Southern Patriot
reporting on a conference on grass roots
cultural revival at Highlander, 1965

"The only place where we could say we did not like slavery, say it for ourselves to hear, was in these old songs. We could not read and the master thought he could trap us with no existence and we could do nothing about it. But we did -- even as children -- with the music. And it is our own; it came from ourselves.

These old-time songs were sung way back when our fore-parents didn't know one note from another. These songs was handed down to them, and we're still singing them the way that they did, and there's people taking note of it.

We're teaching you, telling you where we came from with these songs. Our children, and your children, are all coming on up. They call us the old-time. You know, they'll call y'all old-time someday too. I'm just going to stay old like this and let you people know where those songs you're singing now came from. You get it all so you'll know where the foundation is. You got to know the bottom before you know the top. Then you'll know where you're at.

In my time when I was coming up we had plays -- ring plays of different types. And those old ring plays sometimes meant a whole lot to the people and what they had to say and what they wanted to do. We had a play -- there used to be four of us would stand in a circle and skip across and swing one another:"

Bessie Jones of the Georgia Sea Island Singers speaking at a conference to introduce young freedom workers to root material - Atlanta, 1964.

Throw Me Anywhere, Lord

New words & new music adaptation by Bessie Jones.
Collected & edited with additional new material by Alan Lomax.
TRO © 1972 Ludlow Music, Inc., New York, NY.
International Copyright Secured. Made in USA.
All Rights Reserved Including Public Performance For Profit.
Used by Permission.

'Way back in the old times they made up this buzzard lope. They'd show how the buzzard would go around his prey -- his mule or his horse. In those days they'd throw them out in the fields and woods and things. The buzzard, when he see something dead, he'd hop around it to be sure it was dead -- look at it, step over it, dance around it, and finally pick it up.

So the people felt the same way. When they died they wasn't buried in the beautiful cemetaries like white folks, but they said in their mind that it didn't matter what they did with their bodies. If Jesus could be put in Golgotha field, I can be put in any field -- throw me anywhere -- just so my soul will be saved."

Bessie Jones

When the SNCC Freedom Singers heard this song at a folk festival in the sea islands, they added new verses and sang, "throw me anywhere in that old jail..."

Throw me an-y-where Lord, in that old__ field, Throw_

_____ me an-y-where Lord,__ in that old field.

Throw me anywhere Lord, in that
old field,
Throw me anywhere Lord, in that
old field.

You can beat and bang me, in that
old field,
You can beat and bang me, in that
old field.

Don't care how you do me...
Since my Jesus call me...

Don't care how you treat me...
Since my Jesus need me...

You can kick and stomp me...
You can kick and stomp me...

Throw me anywhere Lord...

Juba

New words & new music adaptation by Bessie Jones.
Collected & edited with additional new material by Alan Lomax.
TRO © 1972 Ludlow Music, Inc., New York, NY.
International Copyright Secured. Made in USA.
All Rights Reserved Including Public Performance For Profit.
Used by Permission.

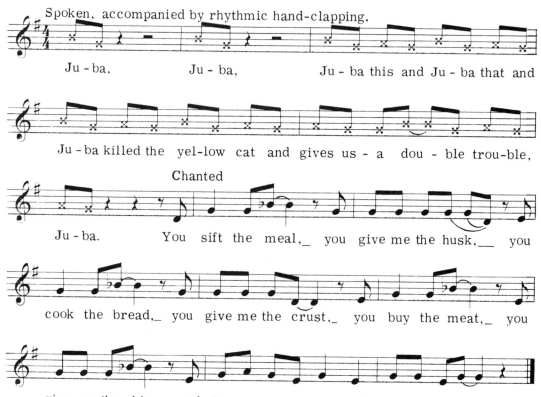

Spoken, accompanied by rhythmic hand-clapping.

Ju - ba, Ju - ba, Ju - ba this and Ju - ba that and

Ju - ba killed the yel-low cat and gives us - a dou - ble trou-ble,

Chanted

Ju - ba. You sift the meal,_ you give me the husk,__ you

cook the bread,_ you give me the crust,_ you buy the meat,_ you

give me the skin,_ and that is where my ma-ma's trou-ble be-gin._

You sift the meal, you give me the husk,
You bake the bread, you give me the crust,
You cook the meat, you give me the skin,
And that's where my mama's trouble begin.

Juba, Juba, you give me double-trouble juba.
Juba-this, and juba-that, and juba killed the yellow cat. *
Juba-up and juba-down and juba all around the town,
Juba.

Massa killed the big old duck and give us all the bones to suck,
Massa killed the big old goose and give us all the bones to chew.

My old massa promised me, when he died he'd set me free.
He lived 'til his head got slick and bald
He give up the notion of dying at all.

*white person

"Juba -- that's giblets. The white people used to pass on the giblets to the colored folk. My grandfather told me when he was a slave they all used to eat out of one big trough. I've seen a trough like that too, so I know it's true.

Give Me The Gourd
To Drink Water

Leader
Reg - u - lar, reg - u - lar roll - ing un - der,_

Chorus ... **Leader**
Give me the gourd to drink wa - ter, Reg - u - lar, reg - u - lar

roll -ing un - der_ Give me the gourd to drink wa - ter.

CHORUS:
Regular, regular, rolling under
Oh, give me the gourd to drink water.
Regular, regular rolling under
Give me the gourd to drink water.

Don't want no gourd for snow water*
Give me the gourd to drink water
Don't want no gourd for snow water
Give me the gourd to drink water.

Oh see what Jesus want with me,
Give me the gourd...
He take me down and set me free,
Give me the gourd....

Well I never seen the like since I
been born....
Well the bull frog's sittin' on the
milk cow's horn...

Oh some of these days and it won't
be long...
Look for me but I'll be gone...

*white people's water

"Someone said that the old people used to sing songs to help themselves, to make themselves feel good anyhow and let the people know that they really knew what was going on. They had feelings.

In the old times they wouldn't let us drink out of a dipper. The white people had glass dippers, but they give us a gourd to drink water, because they figured that a gourd was just right for the colored people. They didn't know the gourd was cool -- cooler than the dipper was. They give us the best thing. We sing a song about it."

Bessie Jones

WORK SONGS

"These songs came from an experience of some thirty years ago in my life when I was a prisoner in the Texas prison system. I had many experiences that are unique only to those who have had the opportunity -- or the curse -- of being a part of the state of Texas house of correction.

These songs came to me at the close of a period in Texas prison life when the mark of a good guard was how cruel or brutal he could be to his prisoners. Usually he was the lowest class of man that could be found -- whose only desire was to get the feel that goes with somebody calling you Boss Man.

There's a man who was known in the prison as Bullyin' Jack-a-Diamonds. He was about 70 years old when I was there. He was assistant captain on the farm and had spent some 35 to 40 years there. He was very cruel. He had a record of killing every man that escaped from his farm. One time thirteen Mexicans escaped and he followed them until he had captured them with the help of a dog. It is reported that he killed the thirteen Mexicans and he was so mad that he shot his horse and put his saddle on his own back and came back to camp."

*Doc Reese, speaking to young
freedom workers at a conference
on Negro folk music at Edwards, Mississippi, 1965.*

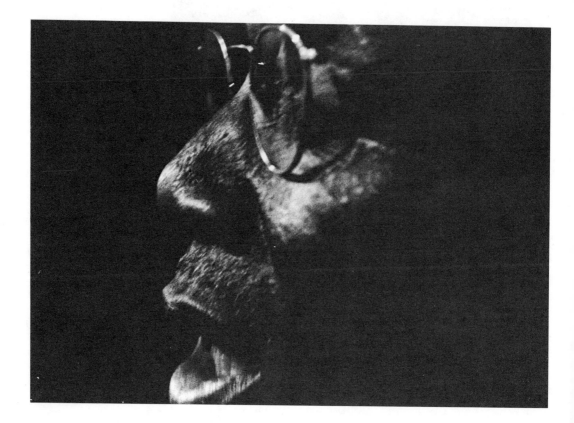

Bullyin' Jack-A-Diamonds

Traditional song as sung by Doc Reese

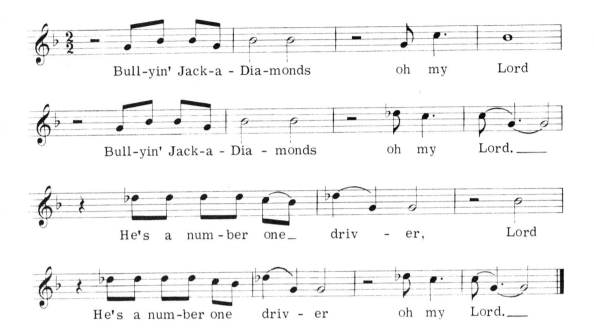

Bull-yin' Jack-a - Dia-monds   oh   my   Lord

Bull-yin' Jack-a - Dia - monds   oh   my   Lord.____

He's a num-ber one_   driv - er,   Lord

He's a num-ber one   driv - er   oh   my   Lord.____

Bullyin Jack-a-Diamonds, oh my
   Lord.
Bullyin Jack-a-Diamonds, oh my
   Lord.

If you walk, he'll drive you, oh my
   Lord, (2x)

He's a number one driver, oh...

He'll drive you to your number,
   oh....

Tell me what is your number, oh....

I have a number like a thousand,
   oh....

I'm a number one roller...

But I'm rocking easy....

I'm rocking but I'm worried...

I'm worried about my baby....
She's driving me crazy...

Tell me what you call your baby...

I call my baby Mary...
I don't believe Jack-a-Diamonds is a
   natural man,
If he was seem like he would understand.

Captain, oh captain, please let me
   down,
I don't believe I can make it for
   another round.

Go Down Old Hannah

Traditional song as sung by Doc Reese

"Every day but Sunday was work day. If it was raining we'd work in the mud -- some eleven miles in a fast trot. The horses was the only thing they was concerned with because they say if you kill a nigger, we'll get another; if you kill a mule we'd have to buy another, so don't kill the mule.

They worked us from the very peak of day until black dark, and would've worked us later but there was a danger of losing somebody. Those who were convicted were always ready; if the boss turned his eye the wrong direction, they were gone.

During this time there were some twenty squads in the field, and there were usually twenty men in each squad. Each squad was guarded by a man who had a six shooter or a Winchester or a double-barrelled shotgun. Each twenty squads had two squads of dogs -- one in front and one behind -- and there were at least two dog sergeants and an assistant captain that followed us wherever we might be working.

Finally at the very close of the day, as the sun began to show herself toward the western horizon, somebody in the field would start 'Old Hannah'."

Doc Reese

Very freely

a) Why don't you go down old Han - nah,

well, well, well, don't you rise no more,—

don't you rise no more,_ Why don't you go down old

Han - nah,_____ Han - nah, don't you rise no more.

a) variant

If you rise in the morn-in', well, well, well,

Why don't you go down old Hannah,
   well, well, well,
Don't you rise no more, don't you
   rise no more,
Why don't you go down old Hannah,
   Hannah,
Don't you rise no more.

If you rise in the morning,
   well, well, well,
Bring judgement sure, bring
   judgement sure,
If you rise in the morning,
   morning,
Bring judgement sure.

Well, I looked at old Hannah, well,
   well, well,
She was turning red, she was...
Then I looked at my partner, partner,
He was almost dead.

You should-a been on this old Brazos,
   well....
Back in 19 and 04,....
You could find a dead man, ...
Layin' across your row.

Why don't you wake up old dead man,
   well...
Help me carry my row,...
   (repeat)

You should-a been on this old river,
   well...
Nineteen and ten,...
You could find them workin'
the women,
and killin' the men.

My mother called me,...
And I answered M'am,...
She said ain't you tired of rolling,...
Rolling for that old sun-down man?

Then my father he called me,...
And I answered Sir,...
He said if you're tired of rolling,...
What do you stay here for.

Then my sister she called me,...
And I answered hey,...
She said ain't you tired of rolling,...
Why don't you run away.

Then my brother he called me,...
And I answered huh,
He said if you're tired of rolling,...
You know you got too long.

I got a letter from the Governor, ...
What do you think he said,...
He said he'd give me a pardon,...
If I didn't frop dead.

Clarksdale, Mississippi
July 5, 1964
10 A.M.

"Hot already. Like Grandmother's kitchen on a summer day when she was heating irons in a tub of coals and cooking on the wood-burning stove at the same time. It is what one would expect, however, in the Mississippi Delta and in Clarksdale, ' the blues capital of the world'.

"I've been traveling through the country that birthed Robert Johnson, Muddy Waters, Charlie Patton, Eli Green, Son House, Skip James, and Fred McDowell. It's flat, except for the trees protruding from the earth occasionally. All one sees is cotton -- from the edge of the highway to the horizon ---- cotton. Sometimes a shack can be seen from the highway, but it merely looks like a different kind of cotton plant. Nothing takes your awareness away from the Delta. It is sky, land and heat ---- each one a plane that stretches interminably and relentlessly. Even the highway is the minimum, the essence of a highway. It is narrow and, unlike the super highways, Highway 61 does not impress itself on the surroundings. Like the blues, The Delta is life in its essentialness. Sky and land. It is one line repeated twice and a rhyming last line --- succint and more than adequate in its expression."

> Julius Lester,
> <u>Blues Pilgrimage: A Mississippi Diary</u>

Delta Blues

Words and Music: Julius Lester
© by Julius Lester 1964
Assigned to Ryerson Music Pub. 1966

I'd rather drink muddy water,
Sleep out a hollow log
I'd rather drink muddy water,
Sleep out a hollow log,
Than to be in Mississippi
Livin' like a dirty dog.

It's down in the Delta,
Cotton up to my front door (2x)
Time the bugs and the white men
   get there
It ain't surprisin' I'm poor.

Thirty cents an hour
And I'm over twenty-one (2x)
And you know my mother told me
That my life had just begun.

Mary had a baby
But I don't believe it's mine (2x)
Baby's got blue eyes
And his hair's just a little too fine.

Tougaloo, Mississippi
July 13, 1964
Early A.M.

"It's raining now and night has emerged from the all-day greyness. Helen and I are drinking bourbon as I show her how to finger an E minor chord. It doesn't matter that she won't learn to play it tonight. It don't matter that she has a difficult time carrying a tune when I don't sing with her. I don't know if I can say what does matter. Maybe the bourbon. It can do something that we can't. It can obliterate the thought of half of a man's body draped over a log in the river. It can make me not care about the 4000 and more lynchings that have occurred in my native land. It can make me forget how long and empty a Mississippi highway is at night; how few houses there are and how many miles of forests there are with dirt roads disappearing into them. How much hate can one individual feel directed at him before his soul fills with a sadness that penetrates even his happy moments?

"She is an old woman and I am an old man and the same trees from which so many Negroes have hung are being washed by the rain tonight. The rain beats on the roofs of the lynched and the lynchers. It soaks into the charred wood of a bombed church and runs down the stained glass windows of another. The grass is green on the banks of the rivers, but when you go fishing take along a winding sheet.

"It is late now and I must sleep. There isn't much any one man can do in this life, but each man should do what he has to and when he has to. Sometimes it is nothing more than making a pilgrimage. Another time it will be nothing more than dying.

'I got to keep moving, I got to keep moving,
blues falling down like hail,
blues falling down like hail,
Uuhh, blues falling down like hail,
blues falling down like hail,
And the day keeps on 'minding me there's a
hellhound on my trail,
hellhound on my trail,
hellhound on my trail.'
— Robert Johnson

"If it must be, so be it."

Julius Lester,
Blues Pilgrimage: A Mississippi Diary

229

Bourgeois Blues

Words & music by Huddie Ledbetter.
Edited with new additional material by Alan Lomax.
TRO © 1959 (renewed) Ludlow Music, Inc., New York, NY.
International Copyright Secured. Made in USA.
All Rights Reserved Including Public Performance For Profit.
Used by Permission.

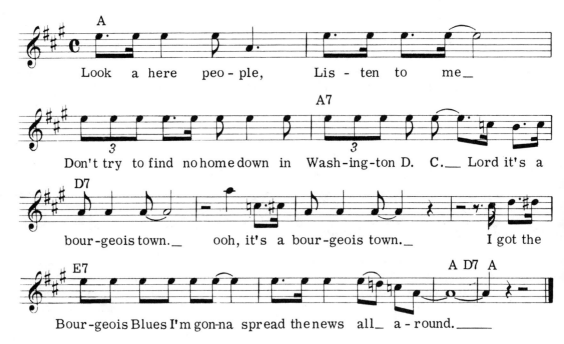

Look a here peo-ple, Lis-ten to me_
Don't try to find no home down in Wash-ing-ton D. C.__ Lord it's a
bour-geois town.__ ooh, it's a bour-geois town.__ I got the
Bour-geois Blues I'm gon-na spread the news all_ a-round._____

Look-a here people, Listen to me
Don't try to find no home down in
　　Washington D. C.

CHORUS:
Lord it's a bourgeois town..... oooh,
It's a bourgeois town.
I got the Bourgeois Blues
I'm gonna spread the news all around.

Me and Martha was standin' upstairs,
I heard a white man say, 'Don't want
　　no colored up there.'

CHORUS

Home of the brave, land of the free,
I don't want to be mistreated by no
　　bourgeoisie.

CHORUS

White folks in Washington, they know
　　how,
Throw a colored man a nickel to see
　　him bow.

CHORUS

Tell all the colored folks to listen to
　　me,
Don't try to find a home in
　　Washington D. C.

CHORUS

Leadbelly, "King of the 12-string guitar," and his songs are recognized not only across the country, but around the world. In Shreveport, Louisiana, however, he is virtually unknown or considered just somebody's old uncle who picked a guitar. Gradually more and more young people in the South, including freedom workers, are hearing about him and beginning to know some of his songs like "Take This Hammer", "Midnight Special", "Goodnight Irene"and "Cotton Fields Back Home".

"...They that walked in darkness sang songs of the olden days -- Sorrow Songs -- for they were weary at heart. There are people who tell us that life was joyous then for the black slave, careless and happy. But not all the past South, though it rose from the dead, can gainsay the heart-touching witness of these songs. They are the music of an unhappy people, of the children of disappointment; they tell of death and suffering and unvoiced longing toward a truer world. In these songs the slave spoke to the world. Such a message is naturally veiled and half articulate.

"Through all the sorrow of the Sorrow Songs there breathes a hope --a faith in the ultimate justice of things. The minor cadences of despair change often to triumph and calm confidence. Sometimes it is faith in life, sometimes a faith in death, sometimes assurance of boundless justice in some fair world beyond. But whichever it is, the meaning is always clear: that sometime, somewhere, men will judge men by their souls and not their skins..."

W.E.B. DuBois, of "The Sorrow Songs"
The Souls of Black Folk, 1903

"SNCC workers identify themselves totally with the people --
the poor, the despised, the downtrodden, the humiliated.
Sharecroppers with eyes, victims with voices, they thrust
themselves into the ditches of desperation so they can speak
more clearly for the inhabitants thereof. "

Lerone Bennett Jr.
SNCC: Rebels With A Cause

"Basically, we're dealing with poor people, and they are the
people we identify with. It even affects our salary scale. One
reason it's so low is just lack of money, but another reason is
that we think you can't come out from a nice hotel every day to
work with these people and then go back at night. Besides, in
Mississippi, as a practical matter, you have to look like a
rural Negro in order to get to talk to a rural Negro. And then
we have to move a lot, and there's no use wearing a coat and
tie if you're likely to end up sleeping on the floor. Another
thing that's operating here too, consciously or unconsciously,
is: Why should we have to comb our hair and put on a coat and
tie to get what are basically our rights? The student sit-in
movement was positive, and without it we couldn't have had
this, but it was also defensive -- to show people we were
clean. This is a different game. Also, there's a certain
mystique about the dress (overalls, rough shoes, etc.), a
certain morale factor. Maybe we've overdone it; it's almost
a uniform now. "

James Forman, SNCC

Down On Me

Traditional, from the singing of
Mrs. Mary Pinckney, John's Island, S.C.

CHORUS:
Down on me, Lord, down on me,
Seems like everybody in this whole
    wide world is
Down on me.

When I get to heaven, gonna sing and
    shout,
Nobody there gonna put me out.
Seems like everybody in this whole
    wide world is
Down on me.

I've been 'buked and I've been scorned
I've been talked about sure's you're
    born.
Seems like. . . .

You can talk about me just as much
    as you please
The more you talk, I'm gonna bend
    my knees.
Seems like. . . .

I Been In The Storm So Long

Traditional, from the singing of Mrs. Mary Pinckney, John's Island, S.C.

I've ___ been in ___ the storm ___ so long ___ You know I've been in ___ the storm ___ so long ___ Sing-in' Oh, Lord ___ give me more time ___ to pray ___ I've been in ___ the storm ___ so ___ long.

* I am ___ a moth - er - less child, ___ Sing - in' I am ___ a moth - er - less child, ___ Sing - in' Oh, Lord, ___ give me more time ___ to pray, ___ I've been in ___ the storm ___ so long. ___

* *This melody most often used for additional verses.*

I been in the storm so long,
You know, I been in the storm so long,
Singin' oh Lord, give me more time to
  pray,
You know I been in the storm so long.

This is a needy time...

Look what a shape I'm in...

Mend all my wicked ways...

I am a motherless child...

Lord, I need you now...

I been in the storm so long...

"Some of us, because we can read a little bit more, forget about the place we came from and some of the songs which motivate us to go on. I remember an old woman who worked on a plantation all her life. Some days she would look up at the sun and sing 'nobody knows the trouble I've seen' or 'I been in the storm so long'. When older folks have sung those songs, it helped them realize they're trusting in God and reaching for a better day.

Regardless of how well a person can sing the classical songs and opera, they don't have that feeling of people who sang from oppressed soul and need. Those songs come from the soul. Even if it was the blues, it's sweet because it comes from a person that is in need for something and is longing for decency and friendship.

Now if we hide those sweet songs and try to get away from what we came from, what will we tell our children about the achievement we have made and the distance we have come?"

Esau Jenkins, Johns Island, S.C.

I'll Be All Right

Traditional - Adapted by food & tobacco workers, Charleston, S.C. 1945

The anthem of the Civil Rights Movement, "We Shall Overcome," was originally a gospel song which came out of the Negro church, known variously as "I'll Be All Right" or "I Will Overcome." It began to evolve into a freedom song as early as 1945 during a food and tobacco workers strike in Charleston, S.C.

"It was a nasty strike, through five and a half months of a rough, rainy and cold winter. It began with 500-600 people, mostly Negroes, picketing every day from 7:30 in the morning 'til 6:30 at night. Eventually people got tired and morale became low. Many people went back to work as the winter turned so cold and rainy.

"To keep up morale, the remaining people would 'sing themselves away' some days. We sang 'I'll be all right...we will win our rights...we will win this fight...the Lord will see us through...we will overcome.' We sang it with a clap and a shout until sometimes the cops would quiet us down.

"Eventually the strike was won on a national level. We were relieved to see the spring of 1946 finally come, and we went back to work."

— Lillie May Marsh, one of the picket captains

Two of the picketers from Charleston took the song to Highlander where it became the theme song. Zilphia Horton carried it all over the south and introduced it to many labor unions. Pete Seeger later took it north and sang it on college campuses. In 1960, Guy brought it to the sit-in movement at the first SNCC conference in Raleigh, N.C.

The variant of the song which appears below comes from a participant in the citizenship school in Wagoner, S.C. We have included in this edition a more authentic early version of the original gospel song that evolved into "We Shall Overcome." That version (which appears on the right hand page) comes from the singing of Mrs. Alice Wine (who is also the source for the song "Keep Your Eyes on the Prize"). It was originally printed in Ain't you got a right to the tree of life? (reprinted by The Univ. of Georgia Press, 1989).

I Will Overcome

I want to be like him . . . etc.

I want to pray like him . . . etc.

I will sing a song . . . etc.

I'll see the king . . . etc.

I want to walk like him . . . etc.

Oh, I will overcome, I will overcome, I will overcome someday,
Lordy, down in my heart, I do believe, I will overcome someday.

"Through song and dance a people are able to share their burden, triumph, sadness and gladness of heart. People sing songs of heroism. They sing songs about the common oppressor or exploiter. The smallest and the greatest desires of a people are brought out in folk music. These songs can be used to draw people together and unite them in one common aim, goal and purpose."

Willie Peacock, who organized the first
Mississippi Folk Festival, 1965

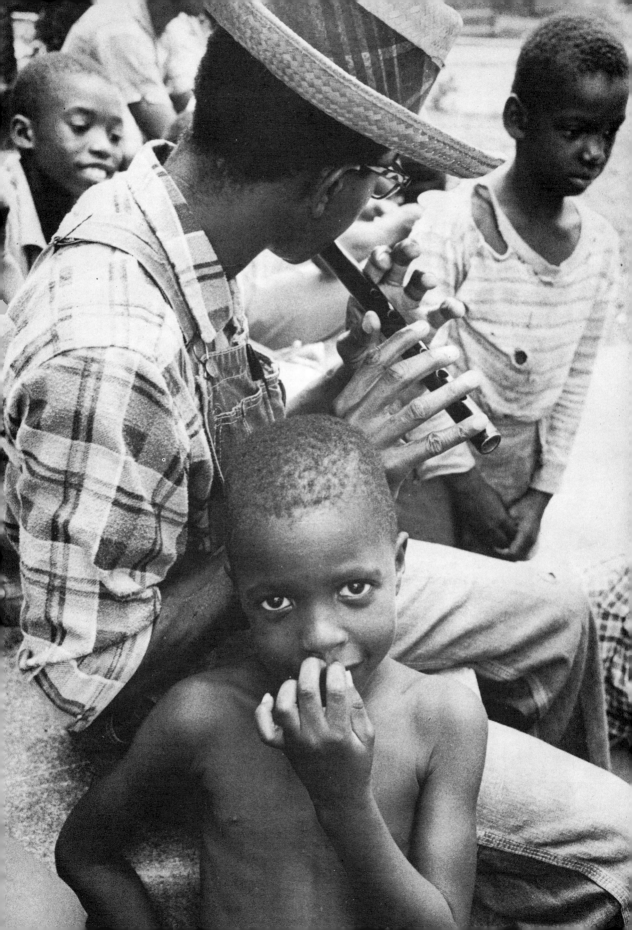

OH, WALLACE, YOU NEVER CAN JAIL US ALL

Selma, Alabama

"We want to live in peace with all mankind, and especially with the whites of the South. Our interests are identical. But we do not want the peace of the lamb with the lion...Give us our rights! Will you do this or force us away from you?"

a Negro minister in Selma, 1887

"Any form of social or educational integration is not possible within the context of our society."

Circuit Judge James A. Hare
Dallas County, 1963

"Selma does not intend to change its customs or way of life."
Chris Heinz, mayor of Selma, 1963

"You're an agitator: that's the lowest form of life."

Sheriff Jim Clark

SELMA, ALABAMA

Selma is the seat of Dallas County, Alabama. In 1961, 57 percent of the population was Negro, but only about 1 percent of the eligible Negroes were registered to vote, while 64 percent of the eligible whites were registered. In the two adjoining Black Belt counties, Wilcox and Lowndes, none of the 11,207 voting age Negroes were registered.

Bernard Lafayette and his wife Colia came to Selma to begin a voter registration drive for SNCC.

"Colia and I first went to Selma in February, 1963. It was sort of our honeymoon; we'd been married about six weeks. The first SNCC worker there came back and said that we might as well scratch Selma off the list because the people there just weren't ready for a movement. We didn't get any different impression when we went there. We had trouble finding a place to live; most people were afraid to put us up. But we work on this assumption: no matter how bad a place is, some people got courage. Those people are gonna be warm and friendly to you.

"It was Mrs. Amelia Bounton who befriended us. We used her office and began to work. The first thing we did was to just try to get people to loosen up, to talk about registration and to realize they needed to vote. We set up classes teaching people how to fill out the registration forms. We knew that the forms are irrelevant in terms of voting and have nothing to do with whether a person is qualified to vote or not. But it's a psychological thing to build people's confidence. They have to feel themselves that they can fill out the form before they feel they can go down to try to register.

"We tried to get people around the city to come, but it was slow. So we went out in the rural. The people out there are close to the earth, they're very religious and warm and friendly. And mostly they're unafraid. They own most of their own property and their little stores. They work hard and they want to see a future for their children. So we got these people to go and try to register to vote first.

"Then we used this as a leverage to try to embarrass many of the people in the city. City folks are sometimes critical and skeptical about country people. So we pointed out that these people were really getting ahead. When these city people began to go down it was really sort of a birth of a movement.

"Between February and September we got about 2,000 people to go down and try to register and about 600 of them actually did get registered.

"By this time we had the people teaching each other. When one person learned to fill out the form, he was qualified to help somebody else. We had recruited some local workers too. We didn't really have to be there anymore.

"We went back to school that Fall. Worth Long and James Love were the SNCC workers who took over in Selma. The situation continued to develop and I would get little bits of news from there.

"In the Fall of 1964 James Bevel and SCLC moved into Alabama and began to build on making Selma a national issue of Voter Registration.

"I went back in 1965 to help with some of the planning and strategy. I saw some great changes. Many, many people had gone to jail -- people you never would have expected to stand up. Some of the kids I had worked with -- whose parents, grandparents and teachers had all argued with them, threatened them and disciplined them -- would run up to me:

"'Guess what happened! Man, my grandmother went to jail! Man, I can't believe it...my grandma's in jail!'

"The principal of one high school who had told the kids he would lower their grades if they participated in the Movement, actually led a march of teachers asking for the right to vote. Many of the informers -- Negroes who used to carry messages downtown to the white people -- were still message-carriers, but they were now bringing messages to us. So I saw a whole city change. Large numbers of adults were participating, both from Selma and from surrounding areas.

"Then when Jimmy Lee Jackson from Marion was killed, I believe that really prompted the march. We realized that the killing would go on, based on people just demonstrating for their right to vote. Somehow we had to make the price of human life go up. People were being shot and killed and the killers were getting off pretty cheap. We felt we had to create what we call 'mass dislocation'. That's a non-violent technique where you make it uncomfortable for people by expressing your grievances in a non-violent fashion. A massive march on Montgomery had been planned for a long time, but no one had set a time-table for it. This seemed like a good time."

Bernard Lafayette, SNCC

Black Sunday at the River of Tears

"Moving on a serpentine path from the low hills of the north, the Alabama River runs crooked beneath the Edmund Pettus bridge, sides along Selma's Broad Street, and drifts languidly on to Montgomery. A large river, it crawls through the dry eucalyptus-dying plants at the water's edge -- worming its slow way through the red Alabama earth.

"There is little beautiful in this river. 'Alabama' is its white name, but to the Negroes of Selma and the Black Belt it is a 'river of tears'. Too many black bodies have stained its muddy waters, too many fathers, brothers, distant uncles -- now misty relations.

"And from the bridge, to the south, the land, surrendering its undulation, begins the long rich submission to the Gulf.

"It is here on this dry dusty 1920's bridge that the marchers came on Sunday. Now it is 'Black Sunday'. They came marching across, black and four abreast like pilgrims to a shrine, pulled together by their fear, massive in their purpose like some ancient Roman column. It is here just past the bridge that they were stopped, black line on the darker asphalt, headed for a vision in Montgomery.

"They knew. They must have known, for to be black and long in Alabama leaves few secrets. They knew as they paused forty seconds and as the rasp 'Troopers Advance' rang out across the dry tension, and they knew at the dull first thud upon the skull of John Lewis.

"The women fell first, for women rarely believe they will be beaten no matter how many times they are. And with the thud of billy clubs, they fell, legs askew, black thighs and legs shining in the sweat of tears. They lay upon the hot pavement and awaited the jolts from fourteen ounces of oak. They fell and even the car-hipped possemen and bellied troopers could catch an old woman. They and the children began to run in circles, and the troopers, predicting their circuits, would stand in wait and club them as they passed.

"The men, lithe, athletic on their feet, escaping at first, saw this and returned to lie across the bodies of the women and the screeching children. With the stage set, the troopers flailed at the living hulks beneath them. And when the bodies relaxed and rolled stunned, the clubs found others, and the strange tableaux, body by body, couple by couple, found its way back across the bridge toward the city.

"It was a quiet mid-spring day. Sheriff James Clark lifted his head toward the wind, methodically set his foot and fired. The bright cannister lofted gently over the heads of the streaming troopers and landed amidst the retreating demonstrators. With a hollow sound more cannisters clanked metallically on the soft asphalt, sprouting the frightening clouds of gas.

"And now, the wounded behind, the body, shucked of those who had scampered down the steep slopes of the river bank, jumped the highway barriers, avoided the hostile whites jeering, and fled across the fields to safety, this group, this body down to its core of those who were unable to run, too dazed, too unconscious to run, would not run, this body was inched back to Selma. Back from the light of the distant goal in Montgomery, back into the world a hundred years ago, back into slavery and injustice, back into Selma, this black crowd was inched, pushed, shoved, beaten, horse-prodded, back across the bridge, down Broad Street, into Sylvan, back to the church where it had begun."

Henry Hampton, <u>To Bear Witness</u>
Unitarian - Universalist Association

On Monday, March 8, 1965 (the day after Black Sunday) Martin Luther King sent telegrams to many religious groups in North America:

"In the vicious maltreatment of defenseless citizens of Selma, where old women and young children were gassed and clubbed...we have witnessed an eruption of the disease of racism which seeks to destroy all...It is fitting that all Americans help to bear the burden. I call therefore...join me in Selma...In this way all America will testify that the struggle in Selma is for the survival of democracy everywhere in our land."

The nation responded.

For many the decision to go to Selma was a difficult one to make. Rev. James Reeb was one of these for he had heavy responsibilities at home in Boston. But by early Tuesday morning he had joined the hundreds of clergymen and others who had responded to King's appeal.

After Tuesday's march Reeb and two more Unitarian ministers ate together in Walker's Cafe, a gathering place for the marchers in the Negro part of town. They left after dark and the street was already deserted. Four white men appeared from across the street and shouted "Hey niggers, hey you niggers!" just before they set upon the three ministers. Reeb was hit with a club over his left ear. "It was a two-handed swing in the style of a left handed batter, and the man's face was intense and vicious,' remembered one of the other ministers.

Forty-eight hours later James Reeb was dead.

251

This May Be The Last Time

Traditional spiritual
New words from Citizenship schools

James Reeb was not the first casualty in Selma. On February 26, Jimmy Lee Jackson was shot point blank in the stomach by an Alabama State Trooper. "A quiet boy whose life had been unmarked and unnoticed except by a few, was marked by history at his death. Alabama Negroes began a protest march down highway 80 from Selma to Montgomery."

Jack Mendelsohn, *The Martyrs*

This may be the last time,
This may be the last time, children
This may be the last time,
It may be the last time, I don't
   know.

It may be the last time we can sing
   together,
May be the last time, I don't know
It may be the last time, we pray
   together,
May be the last time, I don't know.

It may be the last time that we walk
   together....
It may be the last time that we dance
   together...

Berlin Wall

Tune: Joshua Fit the Battle
Words: Selma Young People

*A barricade, tabbed the Berlin Wall, was set up in front of
Brown Chapel by the police, to define the line of restriction.
The marchers were determined to get it down.*

We've got a rope that's a Ber-lin Wall,

Ber-lin Wall, Ber-lin Wall_____ We've got a rope that's a

Ber-lin Wall in Sel-ma Al-a-ba-ma.

We've got a rope that's a Berlin Wall,
   Berlin Wall, Berlin Wall,
We've got a rope that's a Berlin Wall,
In Selma, Alabama.

We're gonna break this Berlin Wall...

We're gonna stay here 'til it fall...

Hate is the thing that built that wall...

Old George Wallace helped build that
   wall...

Love is the thing that'll make it fall...

We're gonna stand up 'til it fall...

We've got a rope that's a Berlin Wall...

Somewhere between 40 and 50 thousand people gathered in Selma to express their indignation of the murders and the injustice of Alabama. For five days they marched in rain and mud, in sunshine and blisters -- fifty miles to Montgomery.

"It's ironic how I got to Selma. I was over at some Jewish friends' house and we were watching this film on television -- Judgement at Nuremburg. It's a powerful film and it ends with this question -- has everybody been captured, or will there be another war? Right after that, they bring on this newsreel showing the people in Selma getting beaten down by the possemen, and people on horses beating the people down. That was just like a crushing blow. So I felt I had to go to Selma and do something, I didn't know what."

Jimmie Collier, SCLC

Do What The Spirit Say Do

Spiritual - new words by young people in Selma

You gotta do what the spirit say do,
You gotta do what the spirit say do,
And what the spirit say do, I'm gonna
   do, Oh Lord
You gotta do what the spirit say do.

You gotta march when the spirit say
   march (2x)
And when the spirit say march, you
   better march, Oh Lord
You gotta march when the spirit say
   march.

You gotta sing...

You gotta moan...

You gotta picket...

You gotta vote...

You gotta move...

You gotta pray
     preach
     shout
     rock
     cool it
     love
     die.

"We were marching along and some old Army guys were calling cadence -- Hup, hip, to your left ... to your left, right, left. I started thinking that left isn't a thing that we want to get. I mean we want to keep up ... we want to go along ... we want to go to Montgomery which is not getting left. Right is an affirmative statement, so I said why don't we accent on the right foot. And so a-right, right, and then you can put together verses and the answers from the group would be right ... right ... right. And so I started singing:"

Len Chandler

Right! Right!

Words & music: Len H. Chandler Jr.

Pick 'em up and lay 'em down (Right! Right!) Pick 'em up and lay 'em down, (Right! Right!) Pick 'em up and lay 'em down,__ (Right! Right!) All the way from Sel - ma town. (Right! Right!)

Pick 'em up and lay 'em down
　Right! Right!
Pick 'em up and lay 'em down
　Right! Right!
Pick 'em up and lay 'em down
　Right! Right!
All the way from Selma town.
　Right! Right!

Oh the mud was deep, Right! Right!
The hills were steep, Right, etc.
Now we've made some level ground
Let Wallace hear the sound

I've been walking so long
I've put blisters on the street
Well I caught the Freedom fever
And it settled in my feet

Did the rain come down
Well I thought I would drown
Then I thought of Sheriff Jim
Something said you'd better swim

"There was a guy named Jim Letherer who had one leg. He went all the way. There was a picture of us in the N. Y. Times and it said something about the last leg of the march. Jim said 'hey Len, make me a verse':"

Jim Letherer's leg got left
But he's still in the fight
Been walking day and night
Jim's left leg is all right

I been walking so long
I got blisters on my feet
Make me want to skip a beat
I been walking so long
My feet done turn to wheels
I don't think no more of riding
I disremember how it feels
Is freedom all.............
Right! Right!

259

Which Side Are You On?

Original verses by Florence Reese, new verses by Len H. Chandler Jr.
© 1946 (renewed) by Stormking Music Inc. All Rights Reserved. Used by Permission.

Observers lined route 80 -- local Negroes who for one reason or another, usually fear of very real reprisals (State troopers and local police were constantly photographing local participants), did not join the march, watched silently or jubilantly, their faces conveying what this march meant to them. Whites also watched, silently or noisily with signs reading "Rent a priest, $5 per day", "Fake Clergy and Beatniks Go Home", etc.

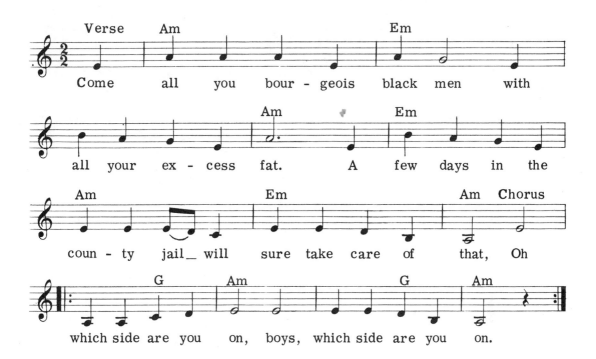

Verse Am | Em

Come all you bour - geois black men with
all your ex - cess fat. A few days in the
coun - ty jail_ will sure take care of that, Oh
which side are you on, boys, which side are you on.

Come all you bourgeois black men
With all your excess fat
A few days in the county jail
Will sure take care of that.

Come all you northern liberals
Take a Klansman out to lunch
But when you dine, instead of wine
You should serve non-violent punch.

Come all you rough, tough bullies
Forget your knives and gun
Non-violence is the only way
The battle can be won.

Come all you high-toned college
   grads
Pronounce your final 'g's
But don't forget your grandma,
She's still scrubbin' on her knees.

Come all you Uncle Toms
Take that hankie from your head
Forget your fears and shed a tear
For the life of shame you've led.

You need not join our picket line
If you can't stand the blows
But join your dimes with dollars
Or be counted with our foes.

I heard that Gov. Wallace
Just up and lost his mind
And he bought a case of Man Tan
And joined the picket line.

They say the Ku Klux Klan
Just up and died their sheets
And now they sing "Oh Freedom"
Everytime they meet.

I've been walkin' so long
I've put blisters on the street
I've caught the freedom fever
And it's settled in my feet.

*For original verses used earlier on the Freedom Rides, etc, see
We Shall Overcome, Oak Publications.

Another Day's Journey

Traditional song - new words SCLC

"I was glad I had on dark glasses because for ten miles, tears were streaming down my cheeks. I just wasn't prepared for the overwhelming feeling of love. I didn't realize that people of every color, every background could really feel together. I was surrounded by Negro teen-agers from Montgomery, wonderful kids with a kind of pride and freedom I'd never seen before. They kept calling to the whites on the sidewalk, 'Come on and join us. We want you too!' And they really meant it."

Price Cobbs, a Negro psychiatrist
from the west coast

Leader (Am)

Well, it's an-oth-er day's__ jour-ney and I'm

Group   Leader (Dm) Group   Leader

glad,_ I'm glad a-bout it, Well, I'm glad, I'm glad a-bout it
                                                    Oh Lord, I'm

(Am) Group   Leader

glad, I'm glad a-bout it, It's an-oth-er day's_ jour-ney and I'm

Group   Leader   (E) (Am)

so glad, I'm glad a-bout it,
                    Oh well_ I'm so glad_ to be here.

LEAD	GROUP
Well it's another day's journey and I'm glad	I'm glad about it
Well I'm glad	I'm glad about it
Oh Lord, I'm glad	I'm glad about it
Well it's another day's journey and I'm so glad	I'm glad about it
Well I'm so glad to be here.	
Well we're going to Montgomery and I'm glad	I'm glad about it
etc.	"
Gonna see Gov. Wallace...	"
I'm gonna tell him I want to be free...	"
Yes, I want the right to vote...	"
It's raining on this road, but I'm glad...	"
Ain't no rain gonna stop me...	"
Ain't no white folks gonna stop me...	"
Ain't no troopers gonna stop me...	"
Well it's another day's journey...	"

Oh, Wallace

"I started singing this song during the summer of 1964. When we walked up to the capitol almost a year later -- about 40,000 people -- it felt good because this made the dream come true."

James Orange, SCLC

dat, They were on their way, da dat__ da da da dat.

CHORUS
Oh Wallace, you never can jail us
    all.... all.... all,
Oh Wallace, segregation's bound to
    fall - da da dada dada da-da-da-da-
    da-da dada dada dada

I read in the paper da da dada dada
Just the other day " " " "
That freedom fighters   etc...
Are on their way
They're coming by bus
And airplane too
They'll even walk
If you ask them to.

Don't you worry about
Going to jail
'Cause Martin Luther King
Will go your bail
He'll get you out
Right on time
Put you back
On the picket-line.

I don't want no mess
I don't want no jive
And I want my freedom
In sixty-five
Listen Jim Clark
You can hear this plea
You can lock us in the house
You can throw away the key.

Now I'm no preacher
But I can tell
You've got to straighten up
Or you're bound for hell
You can tell Wilson Baker
And Al Lingo
That the people in Selma
Won't take no mo'.

Well this is the message
I want you to hear
You know I want my freedom
And I want it this year
So you can tell Jim Clark
And all those state guys too
I'm gonna have my freedom
And there's nothing they can do.

You can push me around
You can throw me away
But I still want freedom
And I want it every day
You can tell Jim Clark
And Al Lingo
It's time for them
To end Jim Crow.

Route Eighty
Is the way we'll come
I know them boys will have
A lot of fun
You might see black
And a few whites too
They're looking for freedom
Like me and you.

I saw James Orange
Just the other day
He was getting ready
To be on his way
He had a white shirt on
And some blue jeans
Just come on to Eighty
You'll see what we mean.

You know Jack and Jill went up the
    hill
And Jill came down with the Civil
    Rights Bill
Don't want no shuckin', don't want
    no jive
Gonna get my freedom in sixty-five.

"It was with great optimism that we marched from Selma to Montgomery. The more than forty thousand pilgrims had marched across a route travelled by Sherman a hundred years before. But in contrast to a trail of destruction and bloodshed, they watered the red Alabama clay with tears of joy and love overflowing, even for those who taunted and jeered along the sidelines. This was certainly a triumphant entry into the 'Cradle of the Confederacy'. And an entry destined to put an end to that racist oligarchy once and for all.

"We had come to petition Governor Wallace. We had come to represent the Negro citizens of Alabama and freedom loving people from all over the United States and the world. We had come not only five days and fifty miles, but we had come from three centuries of suffering and hardship. We had come to declare that we must have our Freedom Now. We must have the Right to Vote; we must have equal protection of the law and an end to police brutality.

"What simple requests. How shameful that American citizens should have to petition a state for such elementary freedoms in the second half of the Twentieth Century. And yet, this was the climax of a three-month campaign, waged at tremendous cost in human suffering including two deaths.

"At the news of still a third murder we were reminded that this was not a march to the capitol of a civilized nation as was the March on Washington. We had marched through a swamp of poverty, ignorance, race hatred and sadism. We were reminded that the only reason that this march was possible was due to the presence of thousands of federalized troops, marshals and a Federal Court order. We were reminded that the troops would soon be going home, and that in the days to come we must renew our attempts to organize the very county in which Mrs. Liuzzo was murdered. If they will murder a white woman for standing up for the Negroes' right to vote, what will they do to Negroes who attempt to register and vote?

"We are reminded that Goveror Wallace was elected by the Klan contingent in the state, and that his administration alone had allowed ten deaths surrounding civil rights activities and twenty-three bombings, with not a single person being convicted.

"And so amidst the joys and triumphs of one of the greatest occasions produced in the ten years of nonviolent struggle, we were called down from the mountain top of hope and exaltation and into the valley of reality, 'a valley of shadow of death'."

Dr. Martin Luther King, Jr.
An Open Letter to the American People

Murder On The Road In Alabama

Words & music: Len H. Chandler Jr.
© 1965 by Fall River Music Inc.
All Rights Reserved. Used by Permission.

"Many people thought a housewife with five children had no business being in Selma at all. Who was looking after the children? Viola Gregg Liuzzo was no ordinary housewife. She was full of energy and independence, a natural 'trouble maker'. When she went to Selma she thought she was serving her family. Her family was mankind.

On the road to Selma today the wheel ruts gouged by Viola Liuzzo's Oldsmobile as it left the highway have been weathered in and grassed over. The four-strand barbed-wire fence, straddled by her car, has been repaired. But not everything is as it was. Someone comes along from time to time and places a small bouquet of field flowers beneath the barbed-wire."

Jack Mendelsohn, *The Martyrs*

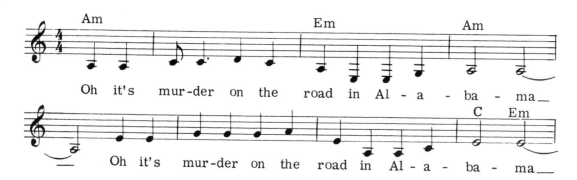

Oh it's mur-der on the road in Al - a - ba - ma
Oh it's mur-der on the road in Al - a - ba - ma

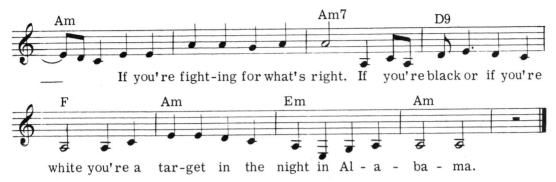

If you're fight-ing for what's right. If you're black or if you're white you're a tar-get in the night in Al - a - ba - ma.

Oh it's murder on the road in Alabama.
Oh it's murder on the road in Alabama.
If you're fighting for what's right,
If you're black or if you're white
You're a target in the night in Alabama.

Oh we marched right by that spot in Alabama (2x)
Oh we marched right by that spot
Where the coward fired the shots
Where the Klansman fired the shots in Alabama.

Oh we know who is to blame in Alabama (2x)
She caught two bullets in the brain
Before we learned to say her name
And George Wallace is the shame of Alabama.

Deep within the sovereign state of Alabama (2x)
Deep within the sovereign state
There's a poison pit of hate,
And George Wallace is the heart of Alabama.

There's a man behind the guns of Alabama (2x)
There's a man behind the guns
Kills for hate, for fear, for fun,
And George Wallace is top gun of Alabama.

It was Jackson on the roads of Alabama
It was Reeb on the roads of Alabama,
William Moore's been dead and gone
But this killing still goes on
Now Liuzzo's on the road in Alabama.

There's a movement on the road in Alabama,
There's a movement on the road in Alabama,
Black man, white man, Christian, Jew
We've got to keep on marching through
Oh the tyrant days are few in Alabama.

It was murder on the road in Alabama. . . .

"The events in Selma demonstrated once more the traditional reluctance of politicians to move unless pressured by a set of disastrous events and an accompanying wave of indignation. President Johnson delivered finally a vigorous speech to a joint session of Congress on behalf of Negro rights, and asked for a strong voting bill to eliminate the subterfuges and schemes used by states to deprive Negroes of the right to vote.

"The bill was passed in late 1965."

Howard Zinn, <u>SNCC: The New Abolitionists</u>

"It is wrong -- deadly wrong -- to deny any of your fellow Americans the right to vote...We have already waited 100 years and more, and the time for waiting is gone...We Shall Overcome!"

President Johnson, presenting the
Voting Rights Bill

WE GOT
THE WHOLE WORLD SHAKIN'

Chicago and the North

It began when police tried to close a fire hydrant that had been opened by Negro youths for relief from 98-degree heat. Fighting broke out and for four days ghetto dwellers used rifles, rocks, bricks and "molotov cocktails" to inflict an untold amount of damage in Chicago's West Side. Finally 4,000 national guardsmen and 1,000 Chicago police armed with machine guns, teargas and orders to "shoot back -- shoot to kill" if they were fired upon put an end to the riot. Two Negroes were dead -- one a 14-year-old girl -- fifty others injured, and more than three hundred had been arrested. When it was over the Chicago black ghetto was about back where it started.

The Negro revolution has spread from the sprawling plantations of Mississippi and Alabama to the desolate slums and ghettos of the North. Like brush fire, riots have spread from city to city. In the summer of 1964 Harlem erupted into violence; in 1965 it was Watts, and in 1966 Chicago's West Side. These were not isolated events. This year the despair of Negro poverty, joblessness, slum housing, inadequate schools, crumbling family life exploded in major cities all across the country. There were out-breaks of violence in Cleveland, Omaha, Oakland, Lansing and Detroit, Brooklyn, Baltimore, San Francisco, Atlanta, Philadelphia and more. No U.S. city is safe from the explosiveness of Negro slums as long as they exist.

In face of this rising violent protest, the leaders of the non-violent movement have charted a course deep into the northern ghettos. Early in 1966 (before violence erupted there) Martin Luther King, Jr. moved his S.C.L.C. staff to Chicago to join forces with local groups in an effort to "End the Slums". As his aide Andrew Young put it, "We have got to deliver results -- non-violent results -- to protect the non-violent movement."

"Our primary objective in this first sustained northern movement will be to bring about the unconditional surrender of forces dedicated to the creation and maintenance of slums and ultimately to make slums a moral and financial liability upon the whole community. We do not hold that Chicago is alone among cities with a slum problem, but certainly we know that slum conditions here are the prototype of those chiefly responsible for the northern urban race problem.

"The Chicago problem is simply a matter of economic exploitation. Every condition exists simply because someone profits by its existence. In a slum, people do not receive comparable care and services for the amount of rent paid on a dwelling. Slum landlords find a lucrative return on a minimum investment. People are forced to purchase property at inflated real estate value. They pay taxes, but their children do not receive an equitable share of these taxes in educational, recreational and civic services. They may receive welfare, but the present system contributes to the breakdown of family life by making it difficult to obtain money if the father is in the houshold. A man or woman may leave the community and acquire professional training, skills or crafts, but seldom is he or she able to find employment opportunities commensurate with these skills. This means that in proportion to the labor, money and intellect which the slum pours into the community at large, only a small portion is received in return benefits. The Rev. James Bevel and our Chicago staff have come to see this as a system of internal colonialism.

"The city administration refuses to render adequate services to the Negro community, and the Federal Government has yet to initiate a creative attempt to deal with the problems of megalopolitan life and the results of the past three centuries of slavery and segregation on Negroes.

"We have chosen to concentrate on each and every one of these issues. We will work on a three phase assault:

"Phase one is based upon the principle that before people can be counted on to act, they must have a full understanding of the 'slum colony' and the resulting slum psychology, which lulls us into a somnolence of despair. The emphasis of this phase will be on education.

"During phase two demonstrations should be scheduled at specific points which reveal the agents of exploitation and paint a portrait of the evils which beset us in such a manner that it is clear the world over what makes up a slum and what it is that destroys the people who are forced to live in a slum.

"Phase three is a phase of massive action. As we begin to dramatize the situation, we will be led into forms of demonstration which will create the kind of coalition of conscience which is necessary to produce change in this country.

"Our objectives in this movement are federal, state and local. On the federal level we would hope to get the kind of comprehensive legislation which would meet the problems of slum life across the nation. At the state level, we should expect

the kinds of tax reforms, updating of building codes, open occupancy legislation and enforcement of existing statutes for the protection of our citizens. On the local level we would hope to create the kind of awareness in people that would make it impossible for them to be enslaved or abused and create for them the kind of democratic structures which will enable them to continually deal with the problems of slum life.

"We would also hope that from this would emerge several pilot projects and institutions which might be of some permanent significance."

Dr. Martin Luther King, Jr.
Winter 1966

277

"The Negro baby born in America today, regardless of the section or the state in which he is born, has about one-half as much chance of completing a high school as a white baby born in the same place, on the same day; one-third as much chance of completing college; one-third as much chance of becoming a professional man; twice as much chance of becoming unemployed; about one-seventh as much chance of earning $10,000 a year; a life expectancy which is seven years shorter, and the prospects of earning only half as much."

John F. Kennedy, June 11, 1963

I Don't Want To Be Lost
In The Slums

Adaption: This Little Light of Mine Chicago Mvmt.

The rea-son I sing this song I don't wan-na be lost, The rea-son I sing this song, I don't wan-na be lost, the rea-son I sing this song, I don't wan-na be lost I don't wan-na be lost in the slum.

The reason I live this life,
  I don't want to be lost,
The reason I live this life,
  I don't want to be lost,
The reason I live this life,
  I don't want to be lost,
I don't want to be lost in the slums.

The reason I sing this song,
  I don't want to be lost...

The reason I join the movement...

The reason I march downtown...

The reason I go to jail...

The reason I sacrifice, Lord.

The reason I fight so hard...

Days of the slums are numbered....

Lost in the slums, Lord...

The reason I live this life...

Lead Poison On The Wall

Words & music: Jimmy Collier

The "End the Slums" Movement can claim its very own talented young composer, Jimmy Collier.

"Little children who are hungry all the time will chew on anything, so they've been eating paint that chipped off their walls. We found out about thirty kids died last year in Chicago from eating lead-based paint. Other children lost their eyesight or suffered brain damage. We got a group of teen-agers together -- kids from off the block -- and they began to cover the community, taking urine samples to spot danger in time and distributing information about lead poisoning. Then with rallies we made it a public issue.

Eventually Mayor Daley put three hundred people to work in the community on the problem, using war on poverty money. Earlier when this plan had been proposed, it was turned down."

Jimmy Collier

Lead poi - son on the wall,__ kills lit-tle guys__ and lit - tle__ dolls.__ It kills 'em big and it

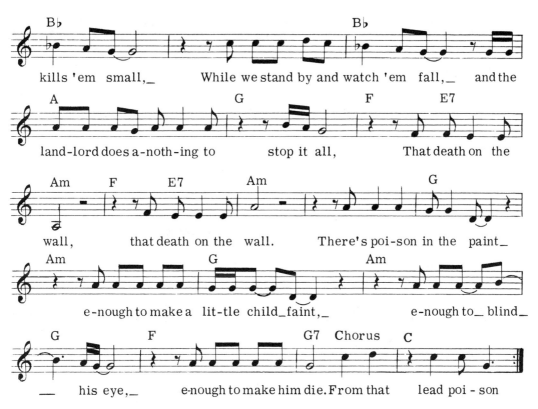

Lead poison on the wall, kills little guys and little dolls,
It kills them big and it kills them small
While we stand by and watch them fall,
And the landlord does nothing to stop it all,
That death on the wall... death on the wall.

There's poison in the paint, enough to make a little child faint,
Enough to blind his eyes, enough to make him die, from the
Lead poison on the wall, kills little guys and little dolls,
Kills them big and it kills them small,
While we stand by and watch them fall,
And the landlord does nothing to stop it all,
That death on the wall.

There's plaster falling from the ceiling,
Plaster falling and plaster peeling,
Doesn't the landlord have any feeling?
Someone's responsible for all that killing, from that
Lead poison.... etc.

Urine samples and knockin' on doors
Label of paint in all of the stores,
Rally and action and you cannot ignore
There's still children dying so we've got do more, on that
Lead poison.... etc.

Rent Strike Blues

Words & music: Jimmy Collier

"Yesterday a twelve month old baby died from a rat bite. The mother picked him up to feed him and the child's eye had been bitten out and he was dead. The landlord justified it by saying, 'well, they don't pick up their garbage. Anyway it was a nigger baby and they have a new one every year, so what does it matter?'

When the city found out about it, they sent some carpenters out to fix the rat-holes. They don't want to face the big problem, they just want to take care of individual incidents."

Jim Letherer, canvassing in Chicago

I got the rent strike, I got the rent strike blues
I got the rent strike, I got the rent strike blues,
Well if the landlord-y don't fix my building
Gonna have to try and move.

Well, I got rats on the ceiling, rats on the floor,
Rats all around, I can't stand it anymore
Going on a rent strike, got to end these blues
Well if the landlord-y don't fix my building
Gonna have to try and move.

I went next door to see my friend,
Landlord won't fix the building and the roaches let me in,
Going on a rent strike, got to end these blues.
Well, if the landlord-y don't fix my building,
Gonna have to try and move.

Well, no fire-escape have we got, no money has the landlord spent,
If he don't fix the building, ain't gonna get next month's rent
Got to go on a rent strike, got to end these blues.
If the landlord-y don't fix my building,
Gonna have to try and move.

Don't care what you do, don't care what you say
Everybody black and white 'titled to a decent place to stay,
Going on a rent strike, got to end these blues
If the landlord-y don't fix my building,
gonna have to try
Gonna have to try,
Landlord-y won't fix my building,
I ain't about to move!

Burn, Baby, Burn

Words & music: Jimmy Collier
© 1966 by Sanga Music Inc. All Rights Reserved. Used by Permission.

"I made up this song while the riot in Watts was going on. I was searching for ways to try and express what I thought these fellows in Watts were trying to say by burning the town down.

We're trying to work with these same type fellows here in Chicago. Most of them think the Movement is kinda square. Their attitude is 'let's tear this town up.' They spend part of their time beating up white people and it's bad because this violence is becoming institutionalized. It's not their fault. It's the fault of the system, because you've got Negro guys growing up now who've never had good experiences with white people, and their families have never had good experiences with white people.

But now Orange* works out with some of them in karate and judo and he can lick 'em all, so they respect his ideas about non-violence.

And with this song, part way through, after they've sung the song and got out some of their hate and some of their vengeance, we try to put in our own pitch about using non-violence to change things. We say you've got to learn, baby, learn, and what you really want to do is build something rather than tear down."

Jimmy Collier

*James Orange - six feet, three inches, 280 lbs. - is a veteran of Alabama and other southern movements.

Mid-dle of the___ sum - mer___ bit-ten by flies and flea Sit-ting in a crowd-ed a-part - ment,___ A-bout a hun-dred and ten___ de - grees___ I went out -side___ _____ The mid dle of the night_____ All I had - a was a match in my hand But I_____ I want-ed to fight___ So I said a burn,___ ba - by, burn,___ Burn,___ ba - by, burn___ ___ No-where to be,___ No me to see (I said a) No-where to turn,___ Burn,__ba - by, burn.___

Middle of the summer, bitten by flies and fleas,
Sittin' in a crowded apartment, about a-hundred-and-ten degrees,
I went outside, the middle of the night
All I had was a match in my hand, but I wanted to fight,
So I said, burn, baby, burn
       Burn, baby, burn
       Nowhere to be, and-a no one to see,
       I said-a nowhere to turn
       Burn, baby, burn.

I called President Johnson on the phone,
The secretary said he wasn't there
I tried to get in touch with Mr. Humphrey
They couldn't find him anywhere.
I went into the courtroom, with my poor sad face
Didn't have no money, didn't have no lawyer
They wouldn't plead my case
So I said, Burn, baby, burn
       etc.

I really wanted a decent job, I really needed some scratch
  (I heard people talking about a dream, now, a dream that I couldn't catch
I really wanted to be somebody and all I had was a match
Couldn't get oil from Rockefeller's wells
Couldn't get diamonds from the mine
If I can't enjoy the American dream, won't be water but fire next time
So I said, Burn, baby, burn
       etc.

Walkin' around on the west side now, lookin' mean and mad
Deep down inside my heart, I'm feeling sorry and sad
Got a knife and a razor blade, everybody that I know is tough,
But when I tried to burn my way out of the ghetto,
I burned my own self up, when I said,
       Burn, baby, burn
       etc.

       Learn, baby, learn
       Learn, baby, learn
       You need a concern
       You've got money to earn
       You've got midnight oil to burn, baby, burn.

I really want a decent education, I really want a decent place to stay
I really want some decent clothes, now,
I really want a decent family
I really want a decent life like everybody else.....

People Get Ready

*"In addition to Jimmy Collier's songs, the 'End the Slums'
movement has adapted many rhythm and blues songs. To
the urban Negro of today, many of these songs provide an
emotional release from the omnipresent suffering, while stimu-
lating the will to struggle, serving them in much the same
manner as the spirituals served their enslaved forefathers."*

*David Llorens, "New Birth in the Ghetto",
Sing Out! July 1966*

Peo -ple get   read - y, there's a   train   a -

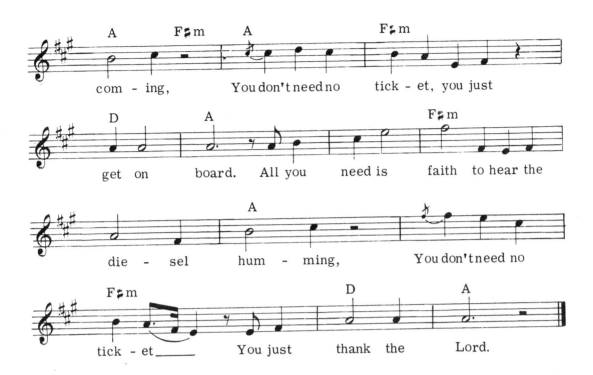

com - ing, You don't need no tick - et, you just get on board. All you need is faith to hear the die - sel hum - ming, You don't need no tick - et_____ You just thank the Lord.

People get ready, there's a train
   a-comin'
You don't need a ticket, just get
   on board.
All you need is faith to hear the
   diesel hummin'
You don't need no ticket, you just
   thank the Lord.

There ain't no room for the hopeless
   sinner
Who would hurt all mankind just to
   save his own (believe me now)
Have pity on those whose chances
   grow thinner
For there's no hiding place when
   the Movement comes.

(Believe me now)
People get ready for the train to
   Freedom
Pickin' up passengers from coast
   to coast.
Faith is the key, open the doors and
   board 'em
There's hope for all among this
   loving host.

Don't want no 'Toms' or any sorry
   Negroes
Comin' to me saying they won't go.
Everybody wants freedom
Everybody, this I know

People get ready for the train a-
   comin'
Don't need no ticket, you just get on
   board.
All you need is faith to hear the
   diesel hummin'
Don't need no luggage, you just thank
   the Lord.

Never Too Much Love

Words & music: Curtis Mayfield (adaptation by the Chicago Movement)

"There's a rock and roll group called the Impressions and we call them 'movement fellows' and we try to sing a lot of their songs. Songs like 'Keep on Pushin', 'I Been Trying', 'I'm So Proud', 'It's Gonna Be a Long, Long Winter', 'People Get Ready, There's a Train a-Comin', 'There's a Meeting Over Yonder' really speak to the situation a lot of us find ourselves in. One song that has really become kind of a favorite with us, especially when we got a lot of mean folks around, is 'Never Too Much Love'."

Jimmy Collier

Chorus:

Too much love,___ too much love,___ nev-er in this world will there be too much love.___ too much love.___ I

Verse:

like to drink whis-key, I like to drink wine, I'd like to have some now, but I just ain't got the time. I got-ta fight for my free-dom, got-ta fight for it now,___ Join___ with the move-ment and we'll show you how.___

CHORUS:
Too much love, too much love,
Never in this world will there be too
    much love.
Too much love, too much love
Never in this world will there be too
    much love.

I like to drink whisky, I like to drink
    wine,
I'd like to have some now, but I just
    ain't got the time.
I gotta fight for my freedom and
    fight for it now
Join with the movement and we'll
    show you how.

CHORUS

I don't know but I think I'm right
Folks in heaven both black and white
I don't know but I've been told,
Folks in heaven won't tell me where
    to go.

CHORUS

*"Now one thing we try to do with this song is to get people
to make up verses. You'd be surprised what kind of verses
come from people who don't consider themselves songwriters
or singers ... Some people don't even consider themselves
people."*

Too much hate, too much hate
Always in this world there is too
    much hate.
Too much war, too much war,
Always in this world there is too
    much war.

War is sad, war is long
Everybody knows that war is wrong,
People tired, people sore,
People just want to end the war.

People in Mississippi thrown off
    their land
Even the government won't give a
    hand.
But the Movement stays on and on
People are living on hope and a song.

If religion were a thing that money
    could buy
The rich would live and the poor would
    die,
But I thank my god it is not so
Both the rich and poor together must
    go.

Some people are good, some people
    are bad,
Some people are happy, some people
    are sad,
Some people are black, some people
    are white,
But we're all together in the human
    plight.

They say the Movement is a non-
    violent thing
Led by people like Martin Luther
    King,
I want my freedom , and I want it
    now
Join with us and we will show you
    how.

Gonna Be A Meetin'
Over Yonder

Words & music: Curtis Mayfield (adaptation by the Chicago Movement)
© 1965 Warner-Tamerlane Publishing Corp. (BMI).
All Rights Reserved. Used by Permission.

*We in the East Garfield Park Community Organization have
been accused of inciting race hatred and attacking white leaders
without just cause. This is a big fat lie. We have never talked
race hatred, but we have attacked the practices of "so-called"
white leaders and with plenty of just cause. They bury their
heads in the sand and ignore the Negro in the slums until he
speaks out against the evils that exist in this community. Some
Uncle Toms want the Negro in the slums to stay in these de-
plorable conditions so that they can continue to draw their fat
checks from the man downtown and ride around in big fine
cars and wear fancy clothes. No matter what boss and his boys
say I still don't like:*

1. *SLUMS*
2. *OVERCROWDED SCHOOLS*
3. *SLAVE WAGES*
4. *A. D. C. **
5. *RATS & ROACHES*
6. *FILTHY ALLEYS*
7. *POLICE HARRASSMENT*
8. *ABSENTEE POLITICANS*
9. *BLACK LACKEYS*
10. *UNINFORMED PEOPLE WHO CRITICIZE
    CONCERNED NEIGHBORHOOD ORGANIZATIONS*

(* aid to dependent children)

*If you want to know what we are doing, come to our next
meeting. All civil rights meetings are open to everybody.
See you any Wednesday at 7:30 P. M.*

*Leo McCord - Citizen of East Garfield
Member of Organization
P. S. FREEDOM*

Children, are you ready?
Gonna be a meetin' over yonder.
Children, are you ready?
Gonna be a meetin' over yonder.
All the boys and the girls gonna
    be there,
And you know the weak and strong
    gonna be there,
Children, are you ready?
Gonna be a meetin' over yonder.

Don't forget to be there
Be at the meetin' over yonder.
Dr. King's gonna be there
Be at the meetin' over yonder.
Don't you know weak and strong
    gonna be there,
The meek and the bold gonna
    be there
Children, are you ready?
Gonna be a meetin' over yonder.

(Keep on pushin' now)

Repeat first verse.

"Young people have made every movement -- from Nashville to Selma..."

"A considerable percentage of the 100,000 unemployed Negroes in Chicago are young men between the ages of 16 and 25. Many of these are in gangs or are drifting idly from corner to corner. This group must be mobilized into an action unit. They must be organized in their own behalf with the focus on meaningful employment and training opportunities through which they might achieve active participation in our society."

Martin Luther King, Jr.

"We have a program of taking teen-agers out to the country on week-ends. We took a bunch of kids up one week-end -- these were supposed to be mean and vicious kids, the gangs you hear about. When we got there they asked us the rules. We had a little session about Negro history, told them about Nat Turner and a few of those folks, and you could see the pride come out on their faces. Then they asked again, what are the rules? So we told them, 'Well, we're going out for coffee and when we come back, you tell us the rules.' We came back in a half hour and they gave us wine bottles, brass knuckles, a few zip guns, knives. They said, 'O.K. first rule is no fighting.'

"The next morning, the kids had a big breakfast. We didn't push them, we let them do what they wanted with their time. So after breakfast they said, 'O.K. we're gonna run for awhile.' This place is a farm with hills. One kid looked out and said, 'Hey man, where's all the houses where all the folks live?' These kids from the ghetto just had no concept that people didn't live crammed up together everywhere.

They started running, and it was beautiful. They ran for an hour and a half -- up and down hills. They'd never had a chance to do that before.

"These kids come back from a session of talking about what's keeping them down, and they lose a little respect for their parents. They want to know how come they never fought the oppression. We don't try to tell them what they can do. We just help them understand what the problems are and then we ask them what they think they can do."

Jim Letherer

Freedom Now

This freedom song is an adaptation by the Chicago Movement of the original composition "Land of a Thousand Dances" by Chris Kenner & Fats Domino Jr., © 1963 Thursday Music Corp. (BMI). All rights are reserved by the original publisher.

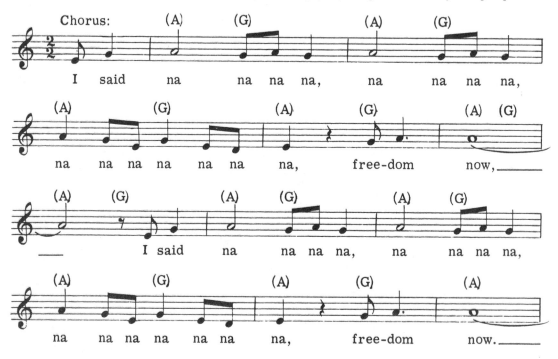

Chorus:

I said na na na na, na na na na,
na na na na na na na, free-dom now,____
____ I said na na na na, na na na na,
na na na na na na na, free-dom now.____

Verse:

_ Do you want your free - dom? Oh yes. Do you

want your free - dom? Oh yes. Do you want your free - dom?

Oh yes. Will you fight for your free - dom? Oh yes.__

I said now - na na na na na na na na na na na na na na na   Freedom now!
I said now - na na na na na na na na na na na na na na na   Freedom now!

LEAD	GROUP
Do you want your freedom?	oh yes
Do you want your freedom?	oh yes
Do you want your freedom?	oh yes
Do you want your freedom?	oh yes
Come on and sing now	oh yes
Sing for your freedom	oh yes
Do you want your freedom?	oh yes
Do you want your freedom?	oh yes

I said now - na na na na na na na na na na na na na na na   Freedom now!
I said now - na na na na na na na na na na na na na na na   Freedom now!

Do you want a job?	oh yes
Then join the movement	oh yes
Do you want education?	oh yes
Then come with me	oh yes
Do you want a home?	oh yes
We're gonna march, children	oh yes
We're gonna end the slums	oh yes
With urban renewal	oh yes
With urban renewal	oh yes
Urban renewal	oh yes
We're gonna stamp out the slums	oh yes

We're gonna do it now - na na na na na na na na na na   Freedom now!
We're gonna do it now - na na na na na na na na na na   Freedom now!

We Got The Whole World Shakin'

This first major experiment with non-violent protest in the North seemed only to inflame whites to riotous anger. As Dr. King and his staff led march after march into working-class white neighborhoods this summer (1966) they were met again and again with a barrage of bricks, bottles and fire-crackers, confederate flags and chants of "nigger, nigger, nigger". On one occasion their cars were overturned and set afire. Dr. King was moved finally to announce that he had never seen such hate -- not in Mississippi or Alabama -- as he saw in Chicago. "We have marched all over the South, but never before have I seen so many people with hatred in their faces and violence in their hearts." He was hit on the head with a rock and jeered and cursed by middle-class whites as he and his marchers protested the imprisonment of a million Chicago Negroes in wretched ghettos and asked for equal access to housing.

Segregationists in the South have predicted for years that when the movement came North people would oppose racial equality as bitterly as they did in the South -- only with more humbug and hypocrisy. Now the time had come and the dire predictions were coming true. When the "race problem" crossed the Mason-Dixon line and encamped in the neighborhoods of the North the result was hysteria and violence in Chicago and other cities -- and retreat and compromise in Congress.

While it had been relatively easy to design and support legislation striking down discrimination in the South, it became impossible to pass a strong bill aimed at open housing in the North.

Verse

We got the_ whole world shak - in' now, some-thing must be go - in' on, (Whole world shak - in'__ Whole world shak - in',) We got the whole world shak - in' now, some-thing must be go - in' on, (Whole world shak-in',) Al - right,_____ (Whole world We got to keep on push - in' just a lit-tle way to shak - in',) go,_____ al - right.____ (Whole world shak-in', whole world shak-in'.)

Chorus

Whole world shak - in' now, Whole world shak - in' now, Whole world shak - in' now, Whole world shak - in' now, Whole world shak - in' now, Whole world shak - in' now,

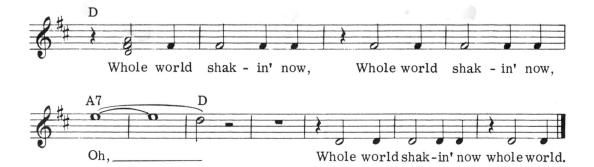

Whole world shak - in' now, Whole world shak - in' now,

Oh,_____ Whole world shak-in' now whole world.

We got the whole world shakin', now
Something must be going on.
We got the whole world shakin'
Something must be going on, all
  right.
We got to keep on pushin'
Just a little way to go, all right.
We got the whole city brimmin'
A movement's going on, all right.
We got the whole city brimmin', now
Got a movement going on.
Oh now, keep on pushin'
Just a little way to go, all right.

CHORUS:
Whole world shakin', whole world
  shakin', whole world shakin' (8x)
Oh.......oh, whole world shakin',
  whole world shakin'

We got the whole world shakin', Dr.
  King is on his way.
Oh, the whole world shakin', Dr.
  King is on his way, all right
We got to keep on pushin', we might
  get our freedom today, all right.

CHORUS

The Chicago Movement vowed to press on in spite of the violence. They temporarily called off the demonstrations when they were able to come up with a ten-point agreement with top civic and business leaders in Chicago. It is a far cry from the "open city" which King and his movement strive for, but it provided a much needed rest from the marches which provoked such violence.

It remains to be seen just how much this movement -- or any northern non-violent movement -- can accomplish. So far the main thing it has done is to expose the racism of a northern city in a highly visible way and to force the entire country to recognize it. The southern campaigns begin to seem almost easy compared to the difficulty of the urban north with its complex tangle of slum-housing, chronic joblessness, poor schools and deteriorating family life. The frustrations and disappointments of Negroes caught in the ghettos of a rich nation are more easily mobilized by riots and angry protest than by the reasoned words of a Martin Luther King.

As Dr. King himself explains:

"Surrounded by an historic prosperity in the white society, taunted by empty promises, humiliated and deprived by the filth and decay of his ghetto home, some Negroes find violence alluring. They have convinced themselves that it is the only method to shock and pressure the white majority to come to terms with an evil of staggering proportions.

"I cannot question that these brutal facts of Negro life exist. I differ with the extremist solution. Our demonstrations, boycotts, civil disobedience, and political action in Negro-white unity won significant victories. In our judgement it remains the method that can succeed. In this conviction the vast majority of Negroes are still with us. In the face of cries of 'Black Power' we helped to summon 60,000 Negroes in the sweltering slums of Chicago to assemble non-violently for protest -- and they responded magnificently.

"The burden now shifts to the municipal, state, and Federal authorities and all men in seats of power. If they continue to use our non-violence as a cushion for complacency, the wrath of those suffering a long train of abuses will rise. The consequence can well be unmanageable and persisting social disaster and moral disaster.

"Negroes can still march down the path of non-violence and interracial amity if white America will meet them with honest determination to rid society of its inequality and inhumanity."

Martin Luther King, Jr.
"Black Power", The Progressive, 1966

"One of the tragedies of the struggle against racism is that up to now there has been no national organization which could speak to the growing militancy of young black people in the urban ghetto. There has been only a civil rights movement, whose tone of voice was adapted to an audience of liberal whites. It served as a sort of buffer zone between them and angry young blacks. None of its so-called leaders could go into a rioting community and be listened to. In a sense, I blame ourselves – together with the mass media – for what has happened in Watts, Harlem, Chicago, Cleveland, Omaha. Each time the people in those cities saw Martin Luther King get slapped, they became angry; when they saw four little black girls bombed to death, they were angrier; and when nothing happened, they were steaming. We had nothing to offer that they could see, except to go out and be beaten again. We helped to build their frustration.

"For too many years, black Americans marched and had their heads broken and got shot. They were saying to the country, 'Look, you guys, we are only going to do what we are supposed to do – why do you beat us up, why don't you give us what we ask, why don't you straighten yourselves out?' After years of this, we are at almost the same point – because we demonstrated from a position of weakness. We cannot be expected any longer to march and have our heads broken in order to say to whites: 'Come on, you're nice guys.' For you are not nice guys. We have found you out.

"An organization which claims to speak for the needs of a community – as does the Student Nonviolent Coordinating Committee – must speak in the tone of that community, not as somebody else's buffer zone. This is the significance of black power as a slogan. For once, black people are going to use the words they want to use – not just the words whites want to hear."

— Stokely Carmichael
"What We Want"
The N.Y. Review of Books, Sept 22, 1966

Move On Over

Words: Len H. Chandler Jr.
Tune: traditional ("John Brown's Body" & "Battle Hymn of the Republic")

Mine eyes have seen injustice in each city, town and state
Your jails are filled with black men and your courts are white with hate
And with every bid for freedom someone whispers to us, "Wait!"
That's why we keep marching on.

CHORUS: Move on over or we'll move on over you (3x)
          And the movement's moving on.

You conspire to keep us silent in the field and in the slum
You promise us the vote and sing us, "We Shall Overcome"
But John Brown knew what freedom was and died to win us some
That's why we keep marching on.

Your dove of peace with bloody beak sinks talons in a child
You bend the olive branch to make a bow, then with a smile
You string it with the lynch rope you've been hiding all the while
That's why we keep marching on.

It is you who are subversive, you're the killers of the dream
In a savage world of bandits it is you who are extreme
You never take your earmuffs off nor listen when we scream
That's why we keep marching on.

I declare my independence from the fool and from the knave
I declare my independence from the coward and the slave
I declare that I will fight for right and fear no jail nor grave
That's why we keep marching on.

Many noble dreams are dreamed by small and voiceless men
Many noble deeds are done the righteous to defend
We're here today, John Brown, to say we'll triumph in the end
That's why we keep marching on.

Keep On Pushing

Words & music: Curtis Mayfield

"Somehow we've got to break down slum conditions and what they do to people. Rats and roaches, overcrowdedness, lack of concern by the landlord -- these things destroy people's motivation, their hope and their vision. The conditions have to be changed and the hold that they have on people must be broken. That's what our Movement is. We say 'End the Slums', but we mean to give life to people who have died because of what the system has done to them."

Jimmy Collier

Keep on _ push-ing, Keep on _ push-ing,

Verse

I've got to keep on _ push-ing, mm _ I

can't stop now. Move up a lit-tle

high - er, Some way, some how,

'Cause I've got my strength and it don't make

sense, Not to keep on _ push-ing _

Hal - le - lu - jah _ Hal - le-

lu - jah,   Keep on _ push - ing.

Keep on pushing... keep on pushing
I got to keep on pushing, I can't
   stop now
Move up a little higher, someway,
   somehow
'Cause I've got my strength, and it
   don't make sense
Not to keep on pushing.

Hallellujah, hallellujah,
Keep on pushing.

Now maybe someday I'll reach that
   higher goal,
I know I can make it, with just a
   little bit of soul.
'Cause I've got my strength, and it
   don't make sense
Not to keep on pushing.

Look-a, look-a yonder, what's
   that I see
A great big stone standing there
   ahead of me.
But I've got my strength, and it don't
   make sense
Not to keep on pushing.

Hallellujah, hallellujah,
Keep on pushing.

Keep on pushing.... keep on pushing...

TITLE AND FIRST LINE INDEX

Titles as they appear in this book are given in regular type. Alternate titles for songs and first lines are given in italics, followed by this symbol (—>) and the title of the song for this book. Songs which have choruses are indexed by the first line of the <u>chorus</u> (rather than the first line of the first verse).

A

Above My Head (B.M.Fikes) —> Up Over My Head 156
Ain't Gonna Let Nobody Turn Me Round 62
Ain't scared a' your jail —> I Ain't... 150
Alabama's got me so upset —> Mississippi Goddam 188
All we ate here —> Alouette (parody) 58
Alouette (parody) 58
And as I cut the weeds —> Father's Grave 176
And the choirs kept singing of... —> Birmingham 122
Another Day's Journey 262
Are you sleeping, Brother Bob? —> Frère Jacques 56

B

Ballad For Bill Moore 104
Ballad of Herbert Lee 96
Ballad of the Student Sit-Ins 40
Banana Boat Song (adap.) —> Freedom's 46
Battle Hymn (Len Chandler adap.) —> Move On Over 307
Battle Hymn of the Republic (Parchman) 55
Been Down Into the South 90
Been in the Storm So Long —> I Been... 236
Berlin Wall 254
Bill Moore —> Ballad for 104
Birmingham jailhouse... —> Bull Connor's Jail 103
Birmingham Sunday 122
Bourgeois Blues 230
Bull Connor's Jail 103
Bullyin' Jack-a-Diamonds 223
Burn, Baby, Burn 284
Buses Are A-Comin', Oh Yes 54
But... —> We'll Never Turn Back 93

C

Careless Love (parody) 56
Carry It On 208
Certainly, Lord 69
Children are you ready? —> Gonna Be A Meetin' 292
Come By Here 87
Come And Go With Me To That Land 68
Come round by my side & I'll... —> Birmingham 122

D

Danville —> Legend of 134
Delta Blues 228
Demonstrating G.I. 136
Did you see Herbert Lee —> Ballad of 96
Dixie (parody) 57
Do What The Spirit Say Do 257
Do you, do you, want your freedom? —> Jacob's 58
Dog, Dog 32
Down by the Riverside (parody) —> Down on the... 58
Down On Me 235

Down in the Valley —> Bull Connor's Jail 103
Down on the Freedom Line 58

E

Everybody Sing Freedom 24

F

Father's Grave 176
Fighting For My Rights 88
Freedom, freedom, freedom's comin' —> Freedom's 46
Freedom in the Air —> Up Over My Head 156
Freedom Is A Constant Struggle 196
Freedom Now 296
Freedom riders... —> Yankee Doodle (parody) 55
Freedom Train A' Comin' 166
Freedom's Comin' & It Won't Be Long 46
Frère Jacques (parody) 56

G

Get On Board, Little Children 86
Get Your Rights, Jack 48
Give Me The Gourd to Drink Water 220
Go Ahead 154
Go Down Old Hannah 224
Go Tell It On The Mountain 204
God's gonna trouble ... —> Wade In The Water 132
Gonna Be A Meetin' Over Yonder 292
Gonna... —> Do What The Spirit Say Do 257
Got on my —> Travelling Shoes 118
Great Day For Me 121
Guide My Feet While I Run This Race 102

H

Hallelujah freedom, hallelujah... —> Been Down 90
Hallelujah I'm A-Travelin' 50
Hammer Song, The 98
Hard Travelin' 106
Hear that... —> Freedom Train A' Comin' 166
Heed the call... —> Ballad of the Student Sit-Ins 40
Herbert Lee —> Ballad of 96
Hit the Road, Jack (adap.) —> Get Your Rights 48
Hold On —> Keep Your Eyes On the Prize 111
How Did You Feel? 22
Hully Gully 53

I

I Ain't Scared A' Your Jail 150
I Been In The Storm So Long 236
I Don't Want To Be Lost In The Slums 279
I got the rent strike blues —> Rent Strike Blues 282
I Know (We'll Meet Again) 37
I Love Everybody 131
I say you, you, —> You Should Have Been There 148
I wanna be ready —> Walkin' For Freedom 78

I Want My Freedom 181
I Want My Freedom Now! —> I Ain't Scared... 150
I want to be like Him —> I Will Overcome 239
I Will Overcome 239
I'd rather drink muddy water —> Delta Blues 228
I'll Be All Right 238
I'm a demonstrating G.I. —> Demonstrating 136
I'm as mild-mannered... —> They Go Wild Over Me 20
I'm Gonna Sit at the Welcome Table 18
I'm On My Way To The Freedom Land 70
I'm So Glad 73
I've been doin' some... —> Hard Travelin' 106
I've got a job —> We've Got A Job 126
If I had a hammer —> Hammer Song, The 98
If you ever go to Jackson —> Midnight Special 58
If You Miss Me From the Back of the Bus 52
It Isn't Nice 182
It was the Student Nonviolent... —> Prophecy 142
It's a bourgeois town —>Bourgeois Blues230
It's Got the Whole World Shakin' (adap.) —> We ... 300
It's... —> Murder on the Road in Alabama 268

J
Jack-a-Diamonds —> Bullyin' 223
Jacob's Ladder (adap.) 58
Juba 218

K
Keep On Pushing 308
Keep Your Eyes on the Prize 111
Kidnapper (adap.) —> Oh, Wallace 264
Kumbaya —> Come By Here 87

L
Land of a Thousand Dances —> Freedom Now 296
Lead Poison On The Wall 280
Legend of Danville 134
Lonely Avenue (adap.) —> Fighting For My Rights 88
Look a-here people, listen to me —> Bourgeois 230

M
Meeting Over Yonder —> Gonna Be a... 292
Midnight Special (parody) 58
Mississippi Goddam 188
Mommy... —> Why Was the Darkie Born? 162
Move on, move on —> Legend of Danville 134
Move On Over 307
Movements Moving On —> Move On Over 307
Moving On 42
Murder On The Road In Alabama 268
My dog a-love-a your dog —> Dog, Dog 32

N
Na, nana, nana —> Freedom Now 296
Never Too Much Love 290
Never Turn Back —> We'll... 93
Never turn back while I run —> Guide My Feet... 102
Ninety-Nine and a Half Won't Do 107
Nothing But A Soldier 152
Now let us sing —> Sing Til the Power... 66

O
Oginga Odinga 138
Oh Bill Moore walked... —> Ballad of... 104
Oh Freedom 74
Oh it's —> Murder on the Road 268
Oh Lord I'm runnin' —> Ninety-Nine and a Half 107
Oh Mary Don't You Weep (parody) 58
Oh Mary, Oh Martha (adap.) —> Oh Pritchett... 64
Oh Pritchett, Oh Kelly 64
Oh riders don't you weep —> Oh Mary... 58
Oh tell me... —> How Did You Feel? 22
Oh, Wallace (You Never Can Jail Us All) 264
Old Hannah —> Go Down, Old Hannah 224
On Top of Old Smokey (parody) 55
One Man's Hands 81
Over My Head (Albany Movement) 77
Over My Head (B. M. Fikes) --> Up... 156

P
Parchman Parodies 55
Paul and Silas bound in jail —> Keep Your Eyes 111
People Get Ready 288
Pick 'em up & lay 'em down —> Right! Right! 259
Pie in the Sky (parody) —> Sweet Bye & Bye 57
Prophecy of a SNCC Field Secretary 142

R
Reason I sing this song, The —> I Don't Want... 279
Regular, regular, rolling under —> Give Me the 220
Rent Strike Blues 282
Right! Right! 259

S
Segregation's been here from... —> Moving On 42
Should-a Been... —> You Should Have Been There 148
Sing Till the Power of the Lord Comes Down 66
St. Augustine —> We're gonna march in... 128
St. James Infirmary (parody) 58
Streets of Laredo (parody) 57
Student Nonviolent Coord. Comm. —> Prophecy 142
Sweet Bye & Bye (parody) 57

T
That's why I'm —> Fighting For My Rights 88
That's... —> Why the Darkie Was Born 162
There's a man by my side walkin' —> Carry It On 208
They Go Wild Over Me 20
They say that —> Freedom Is a Constant Struggle 196
This Little Light of Mine 27
This May Be The Last Time 252
Throw Me Anywhere, Lord 217
Too much love —> Never Too Much Love 290
Travelling Shoes 118

U
Up Over My Head 156

W
Wade In The Water 132
Walkin' For Freedom Just Like John 78
Way down in old Parchman —> On Top of Old... 55

We Are Soldiers 16
We Got A Thing Going On 200
We Got The Whole World Shakin' 300
We Shall Not Be Moved 25
We Shall Overcome 15
We Shall Overcome (orig. version) —> I'll Be All Right 238
We'll Never Turn Back 93
We're gonna... —> Do What the Spirit Says Do 257
We're Gonna March in St. Augustine 128
We've Got A Job 126
We've got a rope that's a —> Berlin wall 254
Welcome Table —> I'm Gonna Sit... 18
Well have you been to jail? —> Certainly, Lord 69
Well I got on my... —> Travelin' Shoes 118
Well I went to Mississippi —> Hully Gully 53

Well it's another day's journey —> Another Day' 262
Which Side Are You On? (J. Farmer) 45
Which Side Are You On? (L.Chandler) 260
Whole world shakin' now —> We Got the... 300
Why don't you... —> Go Down, Old Hannah 224
Why Was The Darkie Born? 162
Wild Over Me —> They Go... 20
Woke Up This Morning With My Mind on Freedom 83
Y
Yankee Doodle (parody) 55
You Are My Sunshine (adap.) —> I Want My Freedom 181
You never can jail us all —> Oh Wallace 264
You Should Have Been There 148
You'd Better Leave Segregation Alone 30
You'll be free, Gradually —> Sweet Bye & Bye 57

PHOTO CREDITS

front cover Ken Thompson
inside front cover Frank Breithaupt
9 Danny Lyons
10 Jim Marshall
13 Jimmy Ellis
14 Bob Zellner
17 Jimmy Ellis
19 Bill Diehl
21 Danny Lyons
23 SNCC
25 H.A. Martin
26 Ida Berman
29 Joe Spieler
31 Bob Zellner
36 Thorsten Horton
41 SNCC
42 Bob Zellner
43 Danny Lyons
44 SNCC
45 Danny Lyons
47 SNCC
49 Billy Barnes
51 Ida Berman
54,55 SNCC
56 Danny Lyons
59 Fred Powledge
61,63 SNCC
67 Fred Powledge
68,69 Bob Zellner
71 Bill Diehl
72,73 Joe Spieler
75 Bill Diehl
76 Ida Berman
79 Thorsten Horton
80 Bill Diehl
81 Bob Adelman
82 SNCC

87 Joe Spieler
89 Bob Adelman
91,92 SNCC
95,97,99,101,102 Danny Lyons
103 SNCC
105 Bob Adelman
109 SNCC
110 Thorsten Horton
113,116 Ken Thompson
118 Matt Herron
120,124-5,130 Ken Thompson
132 Wide World
136 Ken Thompson
140 Daniel Seeger
143 SNCC
146 Ken Thompson
148 Danny Lyon
150,155 Ken Thompson
157 Bob Fitch
160 Ken Thompson
163 Danny Lyon
164,167 Ken Thompson
169 Matt Herron
170,171 Ken Thompson
172 Candie Carawan
173,174,179 SNCC
180 Declan Haun
182 SNCC
184 Ken Thompson
187 SNCC
188,191,194, 195b Ken Thompson
195t Bill Strode
197 Ken Thompson
198 SNCC
203,204 Ken Thompson
207 Fred De Van
208-209 Tom Wakayama

210 Jim Marshall
212 Ken Thompson
215 Robert Yellin
216 Leonard Freed
219,221 Ken Thompson
222 Robert Yellin
226 SNCC
229 Julius Lester
231 Ken Thompson
233 Robert Yellin
234 SNCC
237 Robert Yellin
241 Ken Thompson
242 Ivan Massar
244 Wide World
249 Charles Moore
250 Ken Thompson
252 Willie Squire
255,256 Ken Thompson
260,262, 266b Matt Herron
266t,268,271 Ken Thompson
272 Fred Ward
274 U.P.I.
277,278 Ken Thompson
280 Leonard Freed
283,285,288 Ken Thompson
295 Wide World
296 Ken Thompson
298 N. McNamara (Palmer Agency)
301,305 U.P.I.
309 Ken Thompson